To Jon
From your Grandparents
Yearhas, 2014

SPAIN
in Pictures

VGS

Stacy Taus-Bolstad

Lerner Publications Company

Contents

Lerner Publishing Group realizes that current information and statistics quickly become out of date. To extend the usefulness of the Visual Geography Series, we developed www.vgsbooks.com, a website offering links to up-to-date information, as well as in-depth material, on a wide variety of subjects. All of the websites listed on www.vgsbooks.com have been carefully selected by researchers at Lerner Publishing Group. However, Lerner Publishing Group is not responsible for the accuracy or suitability of the material on any website other than <www.lernerbooks.com>. It is recommended that students using the Internet be supervised by a parent or teacher. Links on www.vgsbooks.com will be regularly reviewed and updated as needed.

INTRODUCTION   4

THE LAND   8

► Topography. Rivers. Climate. Flora and Fauna. Natural Resources and Environmental Issues. Cities.

HISTORY AND GOVERNMENT   20

► Romans and Visigoths. The Moors. Moorish Defeat and Its Aftermath. United Spain. Habsburg Rule. Unrest in the Early 1900s. Civil War and Franco. Emerging Democracy. Government.

THE PEOPLE   38

► Ethnic Identity. Religion. Language. Health. Education.

Website address: www.lernerbooks.com

Lerner Publications Company
A division of Lerner Publishing Group
241 First Avenue North
Minneapolis, MN 55401 U.S.A.

CULTURAL LIFE 46

► Holidays and Festivals. Food. Literature. Music and Dance. Film. Fine Arts. Architecture. Sports and Recreation.

THE ECONOMY 58

► Trade and Tourism. Manufacturing. Agriculture. Transportation and Energy. The Future.

FOR MORE INFORMATION

► Timeline	66
► Fast Facts	68
► Currency	68
► Flag	69
► National Anthem	69
► Famous People	70
► Sights to See	72
► Glossary	73
► Selected Bibliography	74
► Further Reading and Websites	76
► Index	78

Library of Congress Cataloging-in-Publication Data

Taus-Bolstad, Stacy.
    Spain in pictures / by Stacy Taus-Bolstad.
      p. cm. — (Visual geography series)
    Rev. ed. of: Spain— in pictures. ©1997.
    Includes bibliographical references and index.
    Contents: The land — History and government — The people — Cultural life — The economy.
    ISBN: 0-8225-1993-3 (lib. bdg. : alk. paper)
    1. Spain—Juvenile literature. 2. Spain—Pictorial works. [1. Spain.] I. Spain— in pictures. II. Title.
III. Visual geography series (Minneapolis, Minn.)
DP17.T38 2004
946'.0022'2—dc22
                                    2003019638

Manufactured in the United States of America
1 2 3 4 5 6 - BP - 09 08 07 06 05 04

INTRODUCTION

Spain, officially known as the Kingdom of Spain, covers most of the Iberian Peninsula in southwestern Europe. Because of its position at the crossroads between Europe, Africa, and the Mediterranean region, the peninsula has been influenced over the centuries by various groups. People probably first settled on the Iberian Peninsula about 200,000 years ago, and in time, several diverse groups had settled around the peninsula and had established powerful but separate kingdoms.

A unified Spain emerged in the 1400s, when the kingdoms of Castilla y León and Aragón were united through royal marriage. These new monarchs soon united the people under their rule and sought to expand and strengthen Spain's power around the world. In the 1500s and 1600s, Spain dominated the seas and had established many foreign colonies around the globe—including the Americas.

Spain faced several wars, both at home and abroad, over the next two centuries. Though steadily weakening in influence overseas and at home, a succession of monarchs governed into the early 1900s.

Political turmoil let to a bloody civil war in the 1930s. When the war ended in 1939, General Francisco Franco ruled Spain as a dictator until his death in 1975.

After Franco died, Spain's government returned to a monarchy. At the same time, the country made the transition to democracy, establishing a constitution and a parliament to administer its daily government affairs. These changes placed more power in the hands of citizens, and the monarch had very little official power.

The resulting parliamentary monarchy brought political stability and helped Spain's economy grow. Spain's industrial sector flourished. In turn, however, the country's traditional economic mainstay—agriculture—quickly declined. More and more rural people were forced to move to large cities to find work in the new factories, and some even left their homeland to find work in other countries.

At the close of the twentieth century, Spain's economy took a downturn due to rising unemployment and inflation (an increase in

Spain

- — International border
- —·—·— Autonomous region
- ⊛ Capital city
- • City

0 — 100 KM
0 — 100 Miles

N

ATLANTIC OCEAN

PORTUGAL

MOROCCO

Strait of Gibraltar

GALICIA

El Ferrol
La Coruña

ASTURIAS

CANTABRIA

Bay of Biscay

FRANCE

Gulf of Cádiz

Cádiz

Tarifa

CEUTA

GIBRALTAR

MELILLA

Seville

Córdoba

Málaga

Granada

ANDALUSIA

Guadalquivir River

EXTREMADURA

Guadiana River

Tajo River

Astorga

Valladolid

CASTILLA Y LEÓN

Duero River

Ávila

Toledo

Segovia

MADRID

Madrid

Manzanares River

CASTILLA-LA MANCHA

Ciudad Real

MURCIA

Cabo de Gata

Valencia

VALENCIA

ARAGON

Saragossa

EBRO RIVER

Cabo de Tortosa

LA RIOJA

NAVARRA

Pamplona

San Sebastián

BASQUE COUNTRY

Bilbao

Altamira

Reus

Montserrat

Tarragona

Barcelona

CATALONIA

Gerona

Figueres

ANDORRA

Palma de Mallorca

BALEARIC ISLANDS

MEDITERRANEAN SEA

ALGERIA

MOROCCO

0 — 50 KM
0 — 50 Miles

TENERIFE

GRAND CANARY

Las Palma

CANARY ISLANDS

WESTERN SAHARA

prices for goods). Looking to strengthen its ailing economy, Spain's government developed stronger ties to the economy of Europe by joining what eventually became the European Union (EU), an international economic alliance among European nations. Membership in the EU helped boost Spain's economic activity. By the turn of the twenty-first century, the country's economy had rebounded significantly through the development of services and high-tech industries.

Yet ethnic divisions cause tensions in twenty-first century Spain. People from several regions, particularly Basques in the north and Cataláns in the northeast, have long demanded self-rule from the Spanish government. To this end, some groups have turned to terrorism.

After the September 11, 2001, terrorist attacks on the United States, Spain took a stronger stance against domestic terrorism. In 2002 Spanish legislators passed a law banning political parties with alleged ties to the Basque terrorist group Euskadi ta Askatasuna (ETA), which means "Basque Homeland and Freedom."

Internationally, Spain found itself torn between its Middle Eastern oil suppliers and its powerful political ally, the United States. The situation worsened in 2003, when the United States declared war on Iraq. Spain and other U.S. allies were faced with a choice—support the war and lose oil contracts or oppose the war and lose U.S. investment and political support.

Spain's prime minister, José Aznar, publicly supported the war even though an overwhelming majority of Spaniards opposed it. To satisfy his voting public, Aznar refused to offer combat troops from Spain. He did, however, agree to send support for U.S. troops in the form of medical aid.

As Spain continues to develop, the nation's leaders will work to balance economic growth, strengthen the nation's democratic political system, and find solutions to domestic ethnic tensions. With a stable government and economy, this once powerful nation will move with confidence into the twenty-first century.

THE LAND

Spain, located in southwestern Europe, features soaring mountains, vast plains, and long stretches of beautiful coastline. The nation has small fishing villages, large commercial centers, and a variety of agricultural communities.

Bordering Spain to the west is Portugal, the only country that shares the square-shaped Iberian Peninsula with Spain. To the northeast, the Pyrenees Mountains separate Spain from the nation of France. Historically, the border between the two countries has been difficult to cross because of the peaks that straddle the frontier. Andorra, a tiny nation once jointly ruled by Spanish and French officials, is nestled amid the steep slopes. The small British colony of Gibraltar lies near the southern tip of Spain.

Water forms the rest of Spain's boundaries. In the northwestern corner of the Iberian Peninsula, the Spanish region of Galicia fronts the Atlantic Ocean. Spain's eastern and southeastern coasts—from Catalonia in the northeast to Gibraltar in the south—face the Mediterranean Sea.

The Strait of Gibraltar stretches under the country's southernmost tip and links the Mediterranean to the Atlantic. Southwestern Spain looks out over the Gulf of Cádiz, an inlet of the Atlantic ocean.

Spain claims ownership of two offshore island groups: the Balearics in the Mediterranean Sea just off of Spain's eastern coast, and the Canaries in the Atlantic Ocean far to the southwest of Spain. The country controls two cities on the northern coast of Africa—Ceuta and Melilla.

Spain covers a total of 195,363 square miles (505,988 square kilometers), including offshore territories. Altogether, Spain is roughly twice the size of the state of Wyoming.

⊙ Topography

Spain's terrain varies regionally. Mountains extend across the north, while a narrow plain runs southward along the Mediterranean coast. A large plateau stretches across central Spain. The Balearic Islands have gently rolling hills, while the Canary Islands feature volcanic mountains.

Spain's **Canary Islands** feature evidence of volcanic activity, such as this field of solidified lava in Timanfaya National Park.

In Galicia the Cantabrian Mountains rise sharply from the Atlantic coastline. Swift rivers that empty into the ocean have helped to erode the steep, granite slopes of these wet, forested peaks. The Cantabrians reach their highest point in Asturias, a region in north-central Spain.

To the east of the Cantabrian Mountains lie the rugged Pyrenees. These mountains span the French-Spanish border from the Bay of Biscay (an arm of the Atlantic Ocean) to the Mediterranean Sea. Elevations in the Pyrenees vary from 5,000 feet (1,524 meters) to more than 11,000 feet (3,353 m). Numerous streams rush through the mountains, creating picturesque waterfalls that crash down the steep slopes. Because few mountain passes run between the high peaks, major roads and railways cross the border at the coasts rather than in the mountains.

Beginning in Catalonia in northeastern Spain, a narrow coastal plain extends southward and westward along the Mediterranean Sea to Tarifa, a town at the country's southern tip. Along the coast lie many of Spain's most popular vacation spots

ANDORRA

Andorra lies in the heart of the Pyrenees, with a total area of about 180 square miles (466 sq. km). It measures only 16 miles (25 km) from north to south and 18 miles (29 km) from east to west at its greatest distances. Andorra is home to 66,000 people living in about forty towns. The small independent area was jointly governed by both French and Spanish rulers for 700 years. In 1993, however, Andorrans passed a new constitution that placed authority in the hands of its citizens and established an elected parliament. Andorra's economy is based largely on tourism and banking.

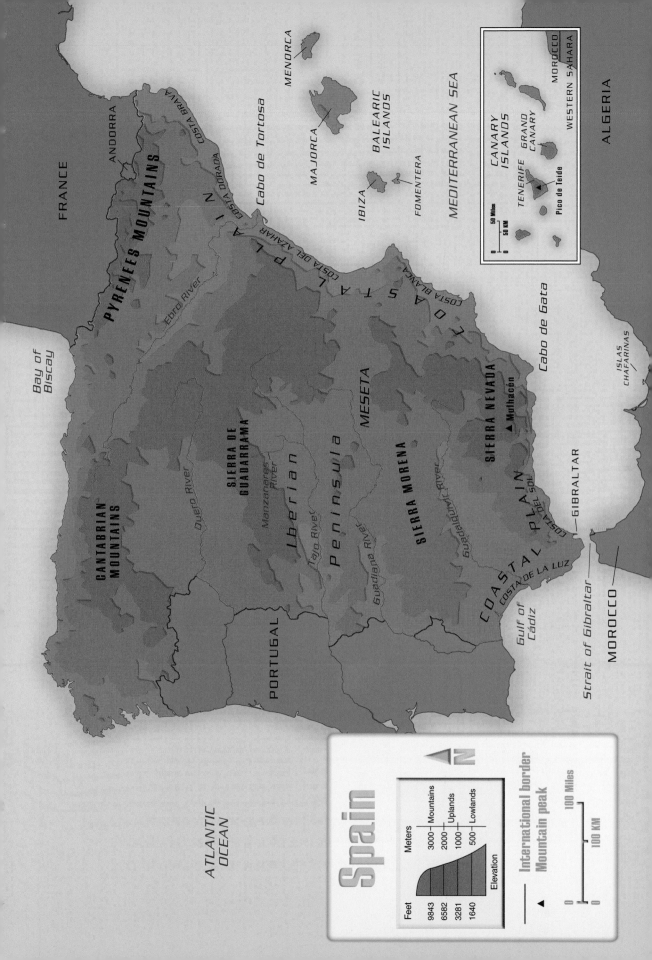

as well as urban centers, farms, and fishing ports. Six different sections of coastland make up the coastal plain region.

In the northeast, the Costa Brava (Rough Coast) runs from the French border southward to the city of Barcelona. The rugged shoreline includes many bays and inlets but few sandy beaches. From Barcelona southward to Cabo de Tortosa (Cape of Tortosa) stretches the Costa Dorada (Golden Coast), named for its gold-colored sands. South of the Costa Dorada is the Costa del Azahar (Orange Blossom Coast), where groves of orange trees abound. Unlike neighboring areas, this quiet section of the coastal plain earns more money from farming than from tourism.

The Costa Blanca (White Coast) begins south of the city of Valencia. The white, sandy beaches of the Costa Blanca extend south to the Cabo de Gata (Cape of the Cat), Spain's southeastern corner. Rounding the corner, the Costa del Sol (Coast of the Sun) makes its

Spain's **Costa Blanca region** contains many sparkling beaches. Visit vgsbooks.com to learn more about Spain's beaches.

way westward to Tarifa. This hot, narrow coast attracts thousands of vacationers year-round. To the west of Tarifa, the Costa de la Luz (Coast of the Light) runs to the Portuguese border. Dazzling white sandbars reach into the Gulf of Cádiz from this section of coastline.

Most of central Spain is covered by the Meseta, a high plateau broken in places by rolling hills and valleys. Steep mountain ranges—the Sierra Nevada, the Sierra Morena, and the Sierra de Guadarrama—rise on the plateau. The Iberian Peninsula's highest peak, Mulhacén, reaches 11,411 feet (3,478 m) in the Sierra Nevada.

The Meseta receives little rainfall and experiences hot summers and cold winters. As a result, the region is difficult to farm. Farmers here grow cereal crops, olives, and saffron. Many people also raise sheep and goats. Although Madrid—Spain's capital and largest city—sits in the center of the Meseta, the rest of the region has a relatively sparse population.

The Balearics, in the Mediterranean Sea, consist of the islands of Majorca, Menorca, Ibiza, and Fomentera, as well as many small islands. The lush vegetation of these low-lying islands includes stands of pines

GIBRALTAR

Gibraltar (above) lies on a narrow peninsula at the southern tip of Spain's coast. Because the Strait of Gibraltar is the only point linking the Atlantic Ocean with the Mediterranean Sea, the area has been an important military and naval outpost for centuries.

Gibraltar was a Spanish territory from the 1300s until 1704, when Sir George Rooke claimed the area for Britain. Spain tried to retake Gibraltar in the 1700s. In 1830 Gibraltar officially became a British colony.

In 1967 and again in 2002, the colony was given the choice to remain a British colony or to return to Spanish rule. Both times, the majority chose to remain under British rule.

Because of its location, Gibraltar has a rich blend of peoples. Gibraltar's citizens are of English, Spanish, Italian, Portuguese, and Maltese descent. The territory's official language is English.

The island of Majorca is a major tourist destination that draws visitors from across Europe and around the world.

and ancient olive and fig trees. Tourism and agriculture sustain the local economy.

About 800 miles (1,287 km) from the Spanish mainland—and 60 miles (97 km) off the northwestern coast of Africa—the Canary Islands dot the Atlantic Ocean. Most of these islands, which are actually the tops of volcanoes, have high central peaks. Their coasts vary from low, sandy shores to steep, rocky cliffs. Spain's highest peak, Pico de Teide, rises 12,198 feet (3,718 m) on the island of Tenerife. Most residents of the Canaries live on Tenerife or Grand Canary—two of the largest islands. The islanders make money from tourism, agriculture, and fishing.

On the North African coast, across the Strait of Gibraltar from the Spanish mainland, lie the cities of Melilla and Ceuta. A Spanish territory since 1497, Melilla was an ancient center of commerce that remains an important port and trading hub. Ceuta has been a Spanish port and military station since 1580. Both cities were given limited self-rule in 1994 but still belong to Spain.

Spain also claims Islas Chafarinas, Peñon de Alhucemas, and Peñon de Velez de la Gomera. These small islands lie off the coast of northern Africa. Morocco contests Spain's ownership of these islands, as well as the Spanish claim to Melilla and Ceuta.

◉ Rivers

In general, the lack of consistent rainfall makes Spain's rivers too shallow for navigation. But several waterways that rise in the mountains collect melting snow in spring. This increased volume powers hydroelectric plants and supplies water for irrigation.

Two major rivers—the Ebro and the Guadalquivir—travel through the Meseta. The Ebro River rises in the Cantabrian Mountains and journeys eastward to the Mediterranean Sea. The river is fed by rushing tributaries that begin in the Pyrenees, where precipitation is plentiful. Irrigation has transformed the broad plains along the riverbanks into fertile farmland. The river's flow, however, fluctuates greatly from season to season.

The Guadalquivir River begins in the Sierra Nevada and runs southwestward through the Meseta into the Gulf of Cádiz. The river basin, a dry but fertile lowland, extends from the foothills of the Sierra Nevada to the coastal plain. Salty marshlands line the southern portion of the river as it makes its way to the sea.

Guadalquivir River

Three other rivers flow westward through the middle of the Meseta. The Duero rises in north central Spain and travels 556 miles (895 km) before emptying into the Atlantic Ocean on Portugal's seacoast. South of the Duero is the Tajo (or Tagus) River, Spain's longest waterway. The Tajo forms part of the Spanish-Portuguese border and flows westward to the Atlantic Ocean. The Guadiana River cuts through south central Spain, turns to the south at the border with Portugal, and empties into the Gulf of Cádiz.

▶ Climate

Spain's climate changes from region to region, with wide variations in precipitation and temperature. The northern mountains are the wettest part of the country and have the mildest temperatures. Cold winters and hot summers characterize the Meseta, while the coastal plains have warm weather year-round. In the winter, snow falls on the northern two-thirds of the mainland and on mountaintops throughout Spain, including those in the Canary Islands.

The northern mountains receive ample precipitation, averaging more than 40 inches (102 centimeters) annually. La Coruña, a coastal city in northwestern Spain, gets more than 30 inches (76 cm) of rain and snow each year. Temperatures near the northern coast are mild throughout the year. La Coruña averages 66°F (19°C) in July, the warmest month, and 51°F (11°C) in January, the coldest month. Inland winters are colder.

Little rain or snow falls on the Meseta. Most of the region gets less than 20 inches (51 cm) of yearly precipitation. Although variations occur, the Meseta's high temperatures hit 80°F (27°C) or more in July, and January's lows dip below 30°F (-1°C). Temperatures in Madrid peak at about 57°F (14°C) during the coldest winter months and soar above 95°F (35°C) in summer.

Like the Meseta, the coastal plains along the Mediterranean are dry. Valencia, on the eastern coast, receives less than 24 inches (61 cm) of rain each year. Temperatures there are mild, although the northern portions are cooler than the southern shores. Winter temperatures average 46°F (8°C) in Barcelona and about 54°F (12°C) in Málaga on the Costa del Sol. Summer temperatures range from 75°F (24°C) in Barcelona to more than 100°F (38°C) on some parts of the southern coast. Spain's offshore islands also benefit from warm, mild temperatures year-round.

◉ Flora and Fauna

In the northern mountains, pine trees, hardy plants (such as edelweiss), and grasses exist at the highest elevations. On lower slopes, evergreens grow alongside oak, ash, and beech trees. Oaks, pines, alders, and willows abound in the mountain valleys and along the coasts.

Evergreens and oaks dot the dry landscape of the eastern coast, and palm trees line the streets of resort areas. The southern and southeastern parts of the coastal plain support orchards of olive and almond trees, and ancient stands of the trees also flourish on the Balearics. Hardy bushes and grasses spring up on the barren plains of the Meseta. Some forests exist at the Meseta's higher elevations, where pine, oak, walnut, chestnut, and poplar trees grow.

A grove of olive trees grows near Málaga in the south of Spain.

Spain's varied terrain makes it suitable for a wide variety of animals, yet its limited forest habitats mean that few large mammals roam the land. Yet brown bears, chamois (a type of antelope), wolves, foxes, and lynx prowl the mountains. Hikers occasionally spot wild boars, mountain goats, martens, and weasels. Snakes, lizards, hares, and rabbits are relatively common in hot, dry areas. Birds include buzzards, Spanish imperial eagles, golden eagles, black vultures, owls, white storks, and pheasants.

Natural Resources and Environmental Issues

Spain is quite poor in natural resources. The Cantabrian Mountains contain deposits of iron ore and some low-grade coal. The country also has small amounts of minerals such as copper, lead, uranium, and zinc. The waters that surround Spain prove a valuable resource for the country. They provide Spain with a strong fishing industry, and resorts along the coasts draw important revenue from tourists.

WHITE STORKS

During January and February, Spain's west and southwest areas become a giant nesting ground for white storks *(above)*. Spain is the first stop on the storks' migration route from Africa to Europe and then back to Africa. The birds often make their large nests atop church towers, trees, or houses.

The country's hot, dry climate and poor soil make farming difficult in most areas and prevent the growth of large trees and green plants in most of the country. In addition, centuries of clearing the land for farming and building have left the Meseta with little more than scrub weeds and grasses. Nearly half of Spain's land area has vegetation, but less than 17 percent of this is forested. Since the 1960s, the government has worked to increase forest covers. But forest fires and uncontrolled harvesting have hindered major reforestation efforts.

Water pollution is an ever-growing problem for the country. The Mediterranean Sea, for example, faces pollution from cities and businesses dumping raw sewage and toxic chemicals into its waters. Oil spills from tankers passing along the country's extensive coastlines have further damaged the country's water and beaches, killing marine life and hurting the tourist industry.

Air pollution presents another environmental problem for Spain. Industry has fast become the driving force in Spain's economy, creating more factories. This in turn, however, means more air pollution, as factories rely on fossil fuels to keep their assembly lines running. In the larger cities, particularly Barcelona and Madrid, more people also means more exhaust and fumes from automobiles. While Spain is working to clean up its air, the growing manufacturing sector and large urban populations make it very difficult to make positive changes.

Cities

MADRID, Spain's capital and largest city, lies almost exactly in the center of the country, near the Manzanares River. Madrid developed into a city around the tenth century and became the capital of Spain in 1561. Madrid has become a sprawling metropolis with 5 million people and is the seat of the federal government. Most of the country's major financial and commercial institutions also have their headquarters in Madrid.

Madrid is a popular city for tourists. Among its splendid historical sites is the Plaza Mayor, a seventeenth-century square surrounded by majestic buildings. Madrid's famous museums include the immense Prado and the Reina Sofia Art Center. The residents of Madrid—or Madrileños—enjoy the city's many outdoor squares, cozy restaurants, and colorful entertainment spots. In 1992 the European Union named Madrid the "Cultural Capital of Europe."

Madrid's Plaza Mayor stands where Arab merchants once set up an extensive marketplace on the bed of a dry lake.

The Barcelona skyline is a mixture of ancient and modern building styles.

BARCELONA, with a population of 2 million people, is Spain's second largest urban center. Lying on the shores of the Mediterranean Sea, this ancient city serves as the capital of Catalonia, a region with its own distinct culture and language. Barcelona has been home to some of Spain's greatest writers, painters, and architects.

Barcelona is Spain's busiest manufacturing city, and its harbor has one of the largest Mediterranean ports. Barcelona's historic importance, unique parks and cultural spots, and impressive layout convinced the International Olympic Committee to choose the city to host the 1992 Summer Olympic Games.

OTHER CITIES Valencia (population 740,000) lies on the Mediterranean coast about 220 miles (354 km) south of Barcelona. Valencia is the capital of a region with the same name. Occupied by Moors from North Africa from the eighth century to the thirteenth century, Valencia has many buildings that reflect this Moorish influence. The city exports citrus fruits from its busy port, which serves the entire region of Valencia. Industry and tourism also add to Valencia's economy.

Seville (population 702,000), another city with a strong Moorish history, serves as the capital of the southern region of Andalusia. Located on the Guadalquivir River, the city has an inland port and is an important industrial hub.

Saragossa (population 603,000), the capital of Aragón, is often referred to as the most Spanish city in Spain, as it is virtually untouched by tourism. Saragossa's old quarter boasts ancient ruins, a Moorish palace, and an important cathedral.

Bilbao (population 358,000) is the largest city in Basque Country. Bilbao is Spain's largest port city and was once heavily industrialized. Due to recent urban-renewal projects, however, the city is fast becoming an important tourist spot. The city's most famous sight is the Guggenheim Museum Bilbao, which features works by many contemporary artists.

HISTORY AND GOVERNMENT

Ancient artifacts found at Gerona, Gibraltar, Valencia, and other sites throughout Spain reveal that early humans probably lived on the Iberian Peninsula by about 200,000 B.C. These early peoples hunted enormous mammoths (elephant-like animals) for food and crafted tools from stone.

In northern Spain, cave paintings such as those at Altamira offer clues about the early Iberians. These paintings, created sometime between 25,000 B.C. and 10,000 B.C., mainly depict hunting scenes, especially bison. Residents of the eastern Iberian Peninsula created rock paintings between 7000 B.C. and 3000 B.C. that show activities such as hunting, fishing, herding, dancing, and even honey gathering.

By about 2500 B.C., Iberian inhabitants were making sturdy buildings and complex tools. The invention of metalworking helped them develop more sophisticated tools. They established fortified hilltop villages, which were scattered over a wide area. This civilization came to be known as Iberia.

The Iberians farmed, mined, and traded with other peoples in the Mediterranean region. The various Iberian settlements evolved in different ways. From the ancient ports of southern Iberia, merchants exported locally mined gold, silver, iron, copper, tin, and bronze. Around 1000 B.C., the wealth of metals in Iberia attracted Phoenician traders from the eastern Mediterranean. They set up a profitable commercial colony from which Iberian metals and other goods—such as salt, dyes, and fish—were transported and sold to eastern Mediterranean markets. A few Phoenician coastal settlements, including Cádiz and Málaga, eventually grew into large cities. Some Phoenicians moved inland to farm.

Meanwhile, explorers from Greece, also in the eastern Mediterranean, were sailing along the southern and eastern coasts of the Iberian Peninsula. Greek colonists founded new settlements, where they minted their own coins and traded with surrounding colonies.

Around 900 B.C., Celts from central Europe began arriving in the northern part of the Iberian Peninsula. Mainly farmers and herders, the

An ancient Celtic spiral etched into the ground in Galicia in northwestern Spain. Spirals were spiritual icons for the Celts.

Celts often intermarried with the Iberian population. The mixing of Celtic and Iberian cultures gave rise to a new group known as the Celtiberians.

As the north flourished, the Phoenician colonies were facing trouble. By the third century B.C., a Phoenician stronghold in the eastern Mediterranean had crumbled. Phoenician leaders from Carthage, a thriving city in northern Africa, assumed control of Phoenicia's Iberian colonies. The Carthaginians planned to use the peninsula as a base for an attack on Rome, a powerful republic on the Italian Peninsula of southern Europe. Recruiting Iberians as soldiers, the Carthaginians invaded Rome in 219 B.C. But the Romans fought back, defeated the invaders, and launched a counterattack. By 206 B.C., Rome had taken control of Phoenician cities on the southern and eastern coasts of Iberia.

◉ Romans and Visigoths

Over the next 200 years, the Romans pushed northward, waging battles against Iberian armies throughout the peninsula. By 19 B.C., Rome dominated all of Iberia.

The Romans called the Iberian Peninsula Hispania. (The name España, or Spain, comes from this.) Roman leaders divided Hispania into provinces and introduced Roman laws and customs. Latin, the language of the Romans, became universal except in the north, where the Basques refused to give up their native tongue.

In the latter part of the first century A.D., the Romans introduced a new religion to Hispania—Christianity. This one-god faith had started in Rome's Middle Eastern provinces in the early first century A.D. Christians follow the teachings of Jesus Christ, who they believe was the son of God. While some Iberians continued to practice their traditional religions, many began to convert to Christianity.

Late in the fourth century A.D., the Roman emperor Theodosius decreed that Christianity would be the empire's official religion. Within a century, most people in Hispania had converted to Christianity.

In A.D. 401, an army of Visigoths, a Germanic group from central Europe, laid siege to Rome. At the same time, other Germanic troops scaled the Pyrenees and conquered Hispania. The Germanic peoples soon began to fight among themselves for control of the peninsula. By the mid-400s, the Visigoths had made deals with Rome to rule kingdoms in Hispania. The Visigoths then drove out all the other Germanic tribes except for the Suebi, who occupied an area in the northwest. The Suebi, as well as the Basques, refused to recognize Visigothic rule.

The Visigothic takeover of the peninsula did not have drastic effects on the Hispano-Roman people because the new rulers worked with Rome. Laws written in Latin were drawn up with the help of Roman leaders. As a result, the Visigoths encountered little resistance. In time, the Visigoths even converted to the Christian religion.

⊙ The Moors

In 711 the Moors, a group from northern Africa, invaded southern Spain and defeated the Visigoths there. The Moors continued north and conquered most of the peninsula by 718. The Moors brought a new language, a new religion, and a new culture to the Iberian Peninsula. They were mainly Arabs and Berbers who spoke Arabic, a language from the Middle East. The Moors were Muslims, or followers of the Islamic religion, which an Arabian prophet named Muhammad had founded in the early seventh century. They called Iberia al-Andalus, meaning "the west" in Arabic. Berbers and Arabs usually occupied separate areas of al-Andalus and often fought against one another for power.

In the southern part of al-Andalus, where the Moors were most dominant, workers built large, ornate mosques (Islamic places of worship) in Córdoba, Seville, Granada, and other cities. Huge

Within a decade of their arrival in Spain, the Moors began building mosques, like this one in Córdoba.

fortified palaces called alcazars housed the Moorish rulers and provided defense against enemy invaders.

Under Moorish control, Arabic was the official language of the
peninsula, and many Christians converted to Islam. A small Jewish
population remained, and another group, called Mozarabs, remained
Christian. Along the northern edge of the peninsula lived groups of
Christians, including Visigothic soldiers and Basques.

From the onset of Moorish occupation, the people of northern
Spain campaigned to retake the peninsula. Christians began an anti-
Moorish crusade known as the Reconquest. As the northern groups
grew, they formed small kingdoms. In one of those kingdoms—called
Asturias—a leader named Pelayo won an important battle against the
Moors in 718. The northern kingdoms expanded southward in the
ninth century, seizing territory in the reconquered lands. At the same
time, Mozarabs from the south were moving to the Christian north.

By 1037 four main kingdoms dominated northern Spain. These
were the kingdoms of Navarra, Catalonia, Aragón, and Castilla y León.

During the Reconquest, northern kings convinced the emirs, rulers
of emirates (small Moorish domains), to pay for protection against their
enemies. Alfonso VI, king of Castilla y León, collected these taxes—
called tributes—but also wanted to add the emirates to his territory. In
1085 his troops conquered the Moorish city of Toledo, an event that

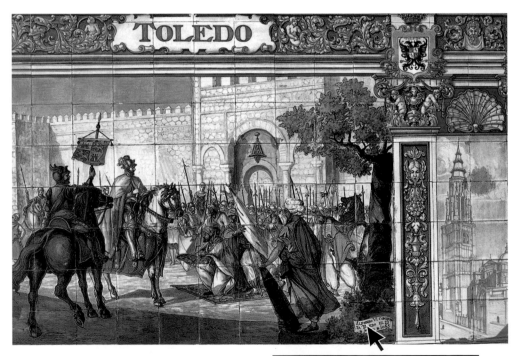

This mural made of ceramic tiles depicts Alfonso VI's troops capturing Toledo
in 1085.

threatened the rulers of other emirates. To fight Alfonso, the emirs requested military support from the Almoravids, a Muslim group from North Africa. The Almoravids journeyed to al-Andalus and stopped the Christian attacks, but they also took over the emirates.

Moorish Defeat and Its Aftermath

During the 1100s, Spain's Christians fought among themselves as much as they battled the Almoravids. The kingdoms shifted alliances with one another through treaties and royal marriages.

Events in North Africa soon gave the northern Spanish kingdoms a chance to rid the peninsula of the Moorish emirates. By the mid-1100s, a Muslim group called the Almohads overthrew the ruling Almoravids and took over the emirates in al-Andalus. By the middle of the following century, however, the Almohad Empire also was crumbling.

By the mid-1200s, Aragón, Catalonia, and Valencia were linked as Christian kingdoms under an Aragónese ruler who controlled eastern Spain. Forces from Castilla y León and Aragón, aided by Portuguese, French, and other armies, chose this time of turmoil to attack. By 1248 the Christian kingdoms had captured all of the Muslim-held territory on the Iberian Peninsula, except for Granada. Because Granada did not pose a threat and its leaders still paid tribute each year to Castilla y León, the Christian kingdoms did not attack it.

In the 1200s and 1300s, peace in the Spanish kingdoms allowed the people to turn their energies toward internal development. Farming, sheepherding, and cattle-raising supported other sectors of the economy. Livestock provided raw materials for woolen goods, and textiles became the chief industry in many towns. Overseas trade also earned money for port cities.

Most of the workers during this time were farmers, but few of them owned the land they worked. Powerful nobles controlled vast areas, and their fields and pastures were tended by peasants (also called serfs). Serfs paid taxes on the food they produced for their own families, owed rent for their homes, and were subject to the rules and orders of the nobles. The nobles enjoyed wealth and a great deal of political power.

This Spanish illustration shows two **noblewomen** playing chess. Many Spanish nobles who lived during the 1200s and 1300s enjoyed lives of leisure, while poor serfs labored in the fields.

THE BLACK DEATH

Outbreaks of plague claimed many lives throughout Europe's history. By far, the worst of these was the Black Death in the 1300s. The Black Death was probably a combination of bubonic plague (spread by insect bites) and pneumonic plague (spread by infected people). The disease originated in Asia and reached southern Europe in 1348, when infected corpses were catapulted by Turkish warriors into a Mediterranean outpost. The plague quickly swept through the Mediterranean area and north into Europe.

It is generally believed that the disease was transmitted from rats to fleas through the insects' bite, then it spread to humans when infected fleas bit people. The plague caused headache, stomach ache, vomiting, fever, and fatigue. Death occurred within two to three days. Before death, however, a victim's skin turned a dark purple—hence the name Black Death. It's estimated that the Black Death claimed 25 million lives in Europe at this time, approximately one-third of the population.

In the mid-1300s, an epidemic of bubonic plague, also called the Black Death, swept through the peninsula, killing large numbers of people and ending Spain's prosperity. Farmlands were abandoned, and their harvests were left to rot. Many businesses closed. In frustration, some Christians blamed their woes on Spain's Jews, many of whom worked as bankers, creditors, and traders. Angry mobs massacred Jews in Valencia in 1391, and similar assaults against Jews occurred later in other parts of the peninsula.

Economic and social problems peaked in Catalonia in the 1400s. The Cataláns felt that their hardships were the fault of the Aragónese monarchy, which spent much of its time quarreling over control of the throne. But the Aragónese ruler, John II, defeated an attempt by the Cataláns to install their own king.

Meanwhile, in 1474 Isabella became the queen of Castilla y León upon the death of her brother. Ferdinand, Isabella's husband, was the son and heir of John II, the king of Aragón. Ferdinand took the throne in 1479, and the kingdoms of Castilla y León and Aragón were united.

◐ United Spain

Castilla y León and Aragón together made up the second most powerful European realm, after France. Although their marriage meant that Castilla y León and Aragón had the same monarchs, Ferdinand and Isabella continued to run them as two separate kingdoms. Political and social conditions in Castilla y León and in Aragón, as well as in kingdoms throughout Europe, had created a large and dissatisfied peasant class. Landowners reaped huge profits from their holdings, while serfs worked for little or no pay. Serfs and low-wage workers could not afford to buy goods and were barred from politics. Many serfs were forbidden to leave the estate without the landowner's consent.

As a result, peasant uprisings became increasingly common and violent. To calm the situation, Ferdinand and Isabella took away much of the nobles' political power. In addition, the monarchs claimed the right to appoint Spain's church officials, who wielded substantial political and social authority. Although these changes resulted in a fairer and more efficient government, the nobles retained most of their economic power.

Religious problems also plagued the newly united Spain. When Ferdinand and Isabella took the throne, the kingdom had large Jewish and Muslim populations. But as a Catholic kingdom, Spain was subject to Roman Catholic law, which viewed all non-Catholics as criminals. Because of this, Spain's Muslims and Jews became the targets for attacks of all kinds.

To carry out the policy of the Roman Catholic Church, Ferdinand and Isabella set up the Inquisition in 1478. Its mission was to expose, expel, or destroy Marranos—Jewish people who had publicly converted to the Catholic faith but who still practiced Jewish traditions in private. By 1492 Inquisition leaders ordered the expulsion of all Jews who refused to be baptized as Roman Catholics. The Inquisition's leaders tortured or killed thousands of non-Christians and seized their property. Many Jews and Muslims fled the country. The Inquisition continued for centuries, until it was finally outlawed in 1834.

Thousands of Spanish Jews were brutally tortured or killed by fire during **the Spanish Inquisition.** Isabella, a devout Catholic, may have set up the Inquisition in an attempt to end heresy (dissent from Church beliefs) in Spain. But experts think that Ferdinand saw the Inquisition as a chance to exterminate Spanish Jews and lay claim to their wealth.

Since Catholicism was Spain's official religion in the 1400s, art from that period often depicts the Moors submitting to Catholics. In this drawing, a Moorish leader surrenders to **Ferdinand and Isabella** after they had captured Granada.

Ferdinand and Isabella also captured Granada from the Muslims in 1492. They gave the Muslims of Granada an ultimatum—convert to Christianity or leave. Although most Muslims agreed to convert, the country lacked Arabic-speaking priests. The converts, therefore, had difficulty learning the Catholic faith.

After conquering Granada, Ferdinand and Isabella concentrated on overseas expansion, especially in North and South America. For example, Isabella provided funding for Christopher Colombus's voyage to the New World. By the early 1500s, Spain's empire included colonies in the Americas that supplied Spain with enormous amounts of silver, gold, and other precious metals. Seville became a major trading center, where ships from the Americas returned with their valuable cargoes. But the money paid to the crown did not begin to cover the costs of running the empire. Though powerful, Spain remained poor.

Habsburg Rule

In 1516 Castilla y León and Aragón passed to Isabella and Ferdinand's grandson, Charles I, who had grown up outside of Spain. Through his father, Charles I was related to the Habsburgs, the royal family of Austria in central Europe. In addition to his Spanish crown, Charles was also crowned Charles V of Austria. He later became the Holy Roman Emperor, leader of a large group of nations in western and central Europe.

Charles I

Because of his many thrones, Charles spent little time in Spain, making him an unpopular monarch there. Revolts flared throughout the kingdom. Unwilling to allow a full-scale revolution, the Spanish nobles joined together to suppress the rebellions. Charles remained in power until 1556, and other members of the Habsburg family ruled Spain after him until 1700.

During the Habsburg reign, wars against other European states consumed Spain's finances and slowed internal development. The monarchy raised taxes and even took property from its citizens to pay its debts. The kingdom's industries did not keep pace with those in the rest of Europe, and the gap between Spain's nobles and peasants continued to widen.

Disagreements over succession led to the War of the Spanish Succession (1701–1714). Charles I had passed the Spanish crown to Philip of Anjou, a member of France's Bourbon dynasty. But Britain, Austria, and other European countries opposed Philip and the extension of Bourbon power beyond France's borders. While these countries invaded Spain to install another Habsburg leader, Catalonia and Aragón revolted against the Bourbons.

THE SPANISH ARMADA

In the 1500s, Spain's navy was one of the most powerful in the world. King Philip began assembling a heavily armed fleet of ships in 1586 to invade England. Once assembled, the Armada (above) had 130 ships and nearly 30,000 soldiers. Philip launched his Armada in 1588 and sailed it to the coast of France. The English filled eight ships with gunpowder, set them on fire, and then sailed them into the Armada. The Armada was forced to sail out to sea, where English ships attacked half of the fleet. The Armada soon retreated, sailing north to round the British Isles, but heavy winds off the coast of Ireland sank many of its ships. By the time Philip's invincible Armada had reached Spain, only 67 of the original 130 ships were left. The fleet was quickly rebuilt, yet its defeat left England in control of the waterways and trade routes to the New World.

During the **War of the Spanish Succession,** Spanish forces were pitted against troops from France, Britain, Austria, and other European nations.

Eventually, Philip—aided by France—defeated his opponents and regained control of the Spanish monarchy. But Spain ceded its European possessions (the Netherlands and colonies on the Italian Peninsula) to Austria and forfeited to Britain some of its trading privileges in the Americas. On the Iberian Peninsula, Britain gained control of Gibraltar. Basque Country and Navarra in northern Spain also remained outside Philip's authority.

During the 1700s, problems with Spain's overseas colonies had a negative impact on the economy. The Americas opened their ports to other European nations, and as a result, the money Spain earned from its colonies sharply declined.

A violent revolution in France further weakened Spain. In 1793 rebels in France executed their king, Louis XVI, and set up a republic (a government of elected representatives). Spain, an ally of the French monarchy, declared war on France's new regime.

In 1799 a military commander named Napoleon Bonaparte seized control of the French government. Napoleon then waged wars throughout Europe. In 1808 his forces invaded Spain, captured several northern cities,

Napoleon Bonaparte leads troops across a Spanish river. Bonaparte invaded Spain in 1808.

and continued to march southwestward. After Napoleon's forces had occupied all of Spain, he gave the Spanish crown to his brother Joseph.

French control of Spain did not last long. Spanish revolutionaries, aided by British troops, forced the French from the peninsula in 1813. Spanish political leaders, collectively called the Cortes, then offered the Spanish crown to Ferdinand VII, a Bourbon heir. The Cortes tried to restrict the king's power and to implement governmental reform, but the Cortes's efforts failed. Spain remained under the leadership of an absolute monarchy, meaning the king had unlimited authority.

Ferdinand's death in 1833 touched off a series of wars between supporters of Queen Isabella, the king's daughter, and Ferdinand's conservative brother Carlos, who also claimed the throne. The conflicts continued until 1868, when Isabella fled the country. Isabella's son Alfonso XII eventually succeeded her. He relied on Antonio Cánovas del Castillo, a shrewd and capable politician, to run the government. Under the leadership of Cánovas del Castillo, Spain enjoyed stability and peace through the late 1800s. But in 1898, Spain fought the United States over Spain's Caribbean colony of Cuba. Spain's defeat in the Spanish-American War (1898) forced the nation to yield its colonies in Guam, Puerto Rico, and the Philippine Islands to the United States. The United States was also given temporary control of Cuba.

Unrest in the Early 1900s

After the war, Spain was a weak, impoverished nation, and the Spanish citizens were pressing for change. Many people in Basque Country and in Catalonia wanted more political freedom. Workers desired laws ensuring better working conditions. Officers in the Spanish army as well as new political parties demanded that their voices be heard.

By the 1920s, the prime minister, political parties, and labor unions had all gained more power and had sharply diminished the role of King Alfonso XIII. But the Spanish people remained divided over how to run the government. The turmoil prompted an army officer, General Miguel Primo de Rivera y Orbaneja, to lead a military revolt against the

Miguel Primo de Rivera y Orbaneja

government in 1923. With support from the king, Primo de Rivera y Orbaneja declared himself prime minister and dissolved the political parties. Ruling through the military, he attempted to control industry, trade, and all parts of the government. He also tried to enact reforms by force.

Primo de Rivera's strict policies angered the army and caused unrest among civilians. To calm the situation, King Alfonso forced the resignation of the prime minister. But civil war still threatened, convincing Alfonso to flee the country in 1930.

Political instability continued. In 1936 the Popular Front, a coalition political party, won national elections. The organization sought to empower the country's working-class people and to fight fascism, a repressive political system led by a dictator and emphasizing extreme nationalism. The Popular Front also separated church and state, lessening the church's role in politics and social systems.

Conservatives in Spain believed that the Popular Front's policies would lead to socialism, a political system based on state ownership of industries, farms, and banks. The conservatives, who thought that a socialist government would greatly weaken the country, began rallying against the Popular Front.

Civil War and Franco

Backed by the Spanish army, the conservatives prepared to overthrow the government. Several officers, including General Francisco Franco, mobilized their supporters and launched a military uprising in 1936. The civil war pitted Franco's forces, called Nationalists, against supporters of the Popular Front, known as Republicans. Internal rivalries among Republican political leaders and a lack of

General Francisco Franco led the Nationalist forces during the Spanish Civil War (1936–1939).

Although the Republican army fought valiantly against Franco's forces, its lack of equipment and leadership led to its defeat.

weapons and ammunition hampered Republican armies. By 1939 Franco's army had seized Madrid, taking control of the government.

Although Franco and the Nationalists had won the war, Spain was nearly destroyed. More than 1 million Spaniards had fled the country, and another 600,000 had died in battle. Franco executed an estimated 400,000 people between 1936 and 1944. Cities, railways, and farmland lay in ruins. Franco had control of a country badly in need of investment and massive rebuilding.

During the 1940s, economic problems hindered Spain's recovery from the civil war. The United States and its Western European allies severed political and economic ties with Spain because of Franco's alliance with the fascist dictators of Germany and Italy. Too few skilled workers, coupled with a lack of investment and with droughts that hurt agricultural production, stalled the economy.

Under Franco's regime, the Spanish people lost many civil and political rights. Franco controlled the press and allowed no opposition to his policies. Censorship kept newspapers and writers from publishing anti-Franco views. His hold on industry and trade fixed wages, froze prices, outlawed labor strikes, and determined which sectors of the economy would be rebuilt.

Franco also restored the Catholic Church as the official religion of Spain and set forth policies that favored the church. It soon influenced the education system and even laws.

During World War II (1939–1945), Franco declared Spain's neutrality, although he openly associated with the Axis powers of Germany and Italy. Britain, France, the Soviet Union, and the United States—

the Allies—eventually defeated the Axis. After the war, the Allies boycotted trade with Axis nations and with Spain. In time, the United States and the Soviet Union became postwar enemies, and the United States sought alliances with other European nations. As a result, the U.S. boycott on relations with Spain ended.

By 1953 the U.S. government was seeking to set up military bases in Europe to counter the forces of the Soviet Union. In exchange for financial support from the U.S. government, Franco allowed American bases to be built in Spain. Additional foreign investment, rising tourism, and industrial growth helped some sectors of the Spanish economy to recover. But rural areas remained poor, prompting farmers to abandon their lands and move to Spain's cities or out of the nation to find work.

As Franco struggled to improve Spain's economy, he faced nationalist uprisings in Catalonia and in Basque Country. In 1959 a few radical Basque nationalists formed the terrorist group called Euskadi ta Askatasuna (ETA). By the mid-1960s, the ETA was staging bombings, assassinations, and other violent activities to press for independence.

The political unrest weakened Franco's hold on power. During the late 1960s and early 1970s, the aging dictator organized the leadership that would follow him. He chose Juan Carlos, the grandson of the last Spanish king, to become his successor. In 1975 Franco died, and Juan Carlos took the Spanish throne.

 To discover more about the Spanish Civil War and the regime of Francisco Franco, go to vgsbooks.com for links.

Emerging Democracy

Contrary to Franco's plans, King Juan Carlos worked with political leaders to map out a transition to democracy. In 1977 general elections were held, and voters chose the members of a two-house legislature. New laws removed many of the repressive measures of the Franco regime and allowed political parties to resurface.

The government developed a free-market economy (a system in which people freely choose what to buy, sell, and make) and encouraged trade and diplomatic relations with foreign countries. To pacify nationalist movements in Catalonia and in Basque Country, Spain granted those regions limited self-rule in 1977. Later, the Balearic Islands, Castilla y León, Extremadura, Andalusia, and Galicia were given similar rights.

In the 1980s, new voices joined the political front. In the 1982 elections, the Partida Socialista Obrero Español (PSOE), or Spanish Socialist Workers Party, came to power under Felipe González. The conservative Popular Party (PP) became the leading opposition party in Spain.

With democratic institutions in place, Spain was able to become more involved in international affairs. In 1982 the nation joined the North Atlantic Treaty Organization (NATO), a military alliance of Western European countries and the United States. In 1986 Spain became a member of the European Economic Community, which later became the European Union, a coalition of nations linked by economic agreements. In 1992 Barcelona hosted the Summer Olympic Games, Seville was the site of the World Expo, and Madrid was honored as Europe's Cultural Capital.

But Spain still struggled with political division, and the PSOE grew weak. In 1993 the ruling party won its fourth general election, and González stayed on as prime minister. But the PSOE had to form an alliance with other political parties to hold its majority in the legislature.

Under González's leadership, the PSOE let go of its socialist positions and shifted its policies to embrace the free-market system. But an economic downturn and soaring unemployment left many Spaniards unhappy with González's government. In 1994 a political scandal spurred many Spaniards to call for González's resignation. Charges of corruption among the PSOE leadership resulted in the arrests and resignations of numerous top government leaders and bank officials. Opposing political parties argued that González should have taken a firmer stance regarding the actions of his socialist colleagues.

In 1996 a new round of elections brought the Popular Party to power. Led by José Aznar, the new government came to power through political alliances. Aznar quickly cut government spending and opened up state-owned economic sectors to private businesses in order to help the ailing economy. By 1998 the economy had improved, and the following year, Spain was eligible to join other European countries that were switching to a new European currency, the euro. The government hoped that this move would strengthen Spain's economy by linking it to other European markets.

While the PP made strides in political and economic realms, it failed to restrain the ETA. Terrorist attacks escalated in 1997 and

On February 23, 1981, Colonel Antonio Tejero attempted a coup d'état by holding parliament at gunpoint for several hours. King Juan Carlos refused to support the rebels in their takeover, and Spain's young democratic system prevailed.

The Basque terrorist group ETA frequently sets off car bombs to threaten the Spanish government. ETA demands Basque independence.

1998. The ETA announced a cease-fire in September 1998, after a series of arrests. The peace ended in 1999, however, and in 2000, assassinations in the name of Basque independence resumed.

Despite this setback, Spain started the new millennium with renewed strength, both political and economic. Aznar won a decided victory in the 2000 elections, and the country also had the fastest-growing economy in the EU. Spain worked to crack down on terrorism after the September 11, 2001, terrorist attacks on the United States, with limited success.

In 2002 Spain officially replaced its long-standing currency, the peseta, with the euro. This moved the country into a more solid position in the European mainstream.

Political and social tensions continued, however, as authorities seized nearly 300 pounds (136 kilograms) of dynamite near Valencia in June. Officials believed that the ETA was planning a strike against tourist resorts along the Mediterranean coast. Throughout that year, Basque bombings continued.

In 2003 Aznar publicly backed a U.S.-led war against Iraq. This move drew criticism from many corners and put his party's leadership on shaky ground. Time will tell if the PP can maintain its majority rule in the Spanish government.

Government

Spain has a democratic form of government called a parliamentary monarchy. Along with a monarch, the leadership includes a prime minister, a cabinet, and a parliament elected by the people. The monarch is Spain's head of state but does not take part in the day-to-day operations of the government. Instead, the monarch advises each administration and represents the nation in international affairs and ceremonies.

Spain's current government was outlined by the 1978 constitution. The prime minister heads the government and presides over the cabinet, a group of officials who decide government policy. Spain's parliament, called the Cortes, includes the 350-member Chamber of Deputies and the 257-member Senate. Members of the Cortes are elected for four-year terms. The political party with the most seats in the Cortes appoints the prime minister. Any Spaniard 18 years or older can vote.

Spain adopted its current constitution in 1978. Spain is divided into forty-seven mainland provinces and three island provinces. Seventeen autonomous regions each have a parliamentary government that decides local issues. Voters in each province elect assemblies, but provincial governors are appointed by the national government. Spanish voters also choose city council members and mayors.

The national government appoints judges who preside over civil and military courts. The civil court system consists of local and provincial courts, appeals courts, and a supreme court. The military courts mostly handle cases involving military personnel and political terrorists.

The Spanish royal family presides over the opening of the Cortes, the Spanish parliament. *(King Juan Carlos stands center, and Queen Sophia sits center.)* The monarch has a largely ceremonial role in government affairs.

THE PEOPLE

From its earliest settlements, Spain has been home to a variety of peoples. Iberians, the early ancestors of modern Spaniards, were joined by Phoenicians and Romans from the Mediterranean, Celts and Visigoths from Western Europe, and Moors from Africa. Each of these groups left their distinct influence on the country's population.

Modern Spain has a population of more than 41 million people. If Spain's population were evenly spread out across the nation, about 211 people would inhabit each square mile of land (81 people per sq. km). In reality, however, most of the population lives along the coasts. The central Meseta, accounting for more than half of Spain's territory, has few inhabitants, and most Meseta dwellers reside in Madrid.

Sixty-four percent of the nation's people live in cities, which are concentrated mainly on the coasts. Two urban centers, Madrid and Barcelona, have populations in the millions. Due to family planning and contraceptive use, the country's population growth rate, which was once very high, has fallen to 0.1 percent. At the current rate, the projected population for 2050 will reach 42.1 million. Despite the lower birthrate, however, Spain's cities are steadily growing.

Most Spaniards lived in the countryside until the 1950s and 1960s, when new factory jobs attracted thousands of rural people to the cities. The cities of Madrid, Barcelona, Valencia, Saragossa, Seville, and Bilbao have the largest metropolitan populations. This influx to cities has created several problems for these areas, however, including over-crowding and air pollution.

Because of the large urban population, most people living in Spain's cities rent apartments in buildings rather than owning their own houses. Urban homes typically have electricity, television sets, and computers. Adults work in a wide variety of jobs, many in factories or professional office buildings.

Many young people living in Spain's cities keep up with the latest in fashion and entertainment, though some older customs remain common. For example, many businesses continue the age-old tradition of shutting down for three hours at midday and reopening in the afternoon, staying open until 7 P.M. Some people take a siesta, or nap, after lunch, though this long-standing custom is no longer widespread.

In rural areas, people often live in villages or small towns. Rural people often live in homes made of clay or stone with tiled roofs. While modern farming methods and equipment have increased yields for farmers, rural people generally have a lower standard of living than city folk. However, most families do own modern conveniences, and many own television sets and automobiles. Many rural families gather in their town's square to visit or to pass the time with games.

Ethnic Identity

Overall, Spaniards share a common culture. Spanish citizens share the Spanish, or Castilian, language and many national traditions. Throughout the centuries, the different groups that have settled in Spain—Visigoths, Celts, Greeks, Romans, and North Africans—have all helped mold the modern nation.

Many Spaniards consider their local ethnic identity to be as important as their Spanish citizenship. In the north, for example, Basque people speak their own language (called Euskera), wear traditional clothing, play locally composed music, host unique celebrations, and prepare regional foods. The Basques are very independent, and in recent times, the Basque independence movement has strengthened the Basque identity.

In Catalonia, traffic signs and posters in shop windows appear in both the Catalán and Castilian languages. Cataláns take pride in the wealth of literature produced in their native tongue. The people of this region also have a reputation as independent and industrious individuals.

Majorcan girls in traditional dress play after church. Spaniards are often more loyal to the traditions of their native region than to national culture.

In the Castilla-La Mancha region in central Spain, Castilians live in sparsely populated towns and villages. Many farm the harsh, arid land. They are considered hardworking and conservative. Their language, Castilian, is the official language of the country.

The Galicians live in the rugged northwest, where they work the land on small farms known as *minifundios*. Many Galicians have moved to other regions in search of more productive farmland, though the region retains its strong Galician influence. Galicians' regional language is Gallego.

Andalusians, who live in the southernmost portion of the country, also possess their own distinct traditions, though they do not have their own language. The Moorish conquest left a strong impression on the region. After the Christian Reconquest, many Andalusians found work on large estates or migrated to other areas in search of work. Andalusians are often considered intense and expressive.

Many of Spain's several hundred thousand Gypsies have adopted the mainstream culture, but some still live in bands that travel from place to place. Some have settled in cities, mainly in Andalusia. Gypsies, who call themselves Roma, speak a

GYPSIES

Gypsies make up a small part of the Spanish population. The name *Gypsy* comes from the Middle Ages, when people believed Gypsies came from Egypt, though they are probably descendants of Indian immigrants. Gypsies often call themselves Roma, and their language is known as Romany. In Spain, Romany has also blended with Spanish and developed into a language called Lengua Calo.

Gypsy families are closely knit and frequently include multiple generations. Gypsies are stereotyped as thieves and cheats, and many Spaniards discriminate against them based on this belief.

language called Romany. Influenced by various musical traditions, the Gypsies created the popular flamenco, a lively, whirling dance performed to guitar melodies, singing, foot stomping, and percussive rhythms.

Religion

The Roman Catholic Church has a long history in Spain, and Catholicism remains the predominant religion there. For centuries, the church played a large role in the culture and lives of the Spanish people. The church enjoyed substantial political power and was supported financially by the country's monarchy.

Nearly 95 percent of the population belongs to the Roman Catholic Church. Church attendance has declined in recent years, however, particularly among younger Spaniards. However, Catholicism remains an important part of Spanish culture. Many of the country's holidays and festivals are based on Roman Catholic traditions, and most people still celebrate important events such as baptism, marriage, and communion within the Catholic Church.

Although it is no longer the official state religion, Roman Catholicism is still very influential in modern Spanish culture.

Most of Spain's non-Catholics belong to the Protestant faith. The Church of the Brethren, the Evangelical Baptist Church, the Jehovah's Witnesses, the Seventh-Day Adventists, and the Mormon church all have followings in Spain. Despite its history of religious persecution, Spain also has a small Jewish population and a small number of Muslims.

Language

Castilian Spanish (from the regional name Castilla) is the official national language. Almost all Spaniards speak it, and the language is taught in most schools. Modern Spanish developed from Latin, the language of the Roman Empire. Pronunciation varies from region to region.

Many English words come from the Spanish language. Some of these include *alligator*, *cargo*, *cork*, *mosquito*, *ranch*, *tomato*, and *vanilla*. In addition, many U.S. places have Spanish names— the states of California, Florida, and Nevada, as well as the cities of San Francisco and Los Angeles, are a few examples.

In addition to Castilian, each region has its own official language. Catalán is spoken in Catalonia, Valencia, and Aragón. Gallego, which is very similar to Portuguese, is used in Galicia. In the Basque community, many people speak Euskera. Catalán and Gallego are rooted in Latin, while the origins of Euskera remain unknown.

About one-third of all Spaniards speak one of these regional languages in addition to Castilian. Because many people are bilingual, most schools in these regions hold classes in both the local language and Castilian. In other parts of Spain, Castilian dialects exist with distinct pronunciations and varying vocabularies.

Health

Spain's healthcare system is good, especially in the larger cities. Nearly all of the country's citizens have access to health services through the government-run public clinics and hospitals. The National Institute of Health oversees the country's healthcare system. Low-income families may receive free medication and dental care.

Health services also are offered through a number of private and church-run hospitals and local Red Cross facilities. Some people buy private insurance. But only an estimated 15 percent of the population has private health insurance, often as a supplement to the public care. While patients have the right to free medical services, they must pay around 40 percent of the cost of prescription drugs.

Workers and their employers contribute to a mandatory health insurance program that covers the costs of hospitalization, tests, and

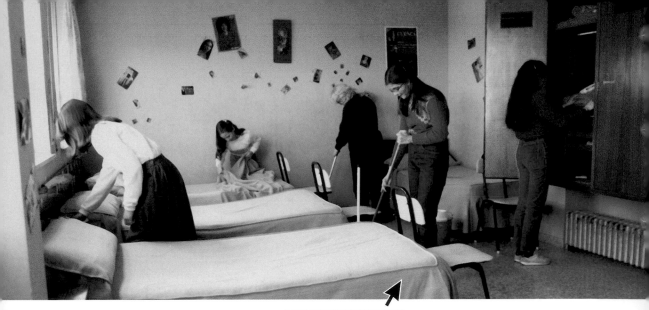

These young women living at a **school for the blind** in Alicante are some of the recipients of National Institute of Health benefits.

routine care. Jobholders receive a portion of their wages when they miss work because of illness or maternity leave. Workers, their employers, and the government also pay for a social security program, which takes care of people who are unemployed, disabled, or retired. The government is encouraging the development of the private insurance sector, however, and in 1999, the country allowed tax breaks for those companies who chose to offer private health insurance to employees.

Spain has about eight hundred hospitals, half of which are private. The central government has allowed the autonomous regions to organize and administer their own health systems. Each administrative region has at least one well-equipped public hospital that provides specialized services. Patients who need treatment at these hospitals must receive a referral from their primary physicians before admittance. Federal money is granted to each autonomous region, based on population. The result is a wide variation among regions in staff numbers and services.

Partly because of this broad-based healthcare system, Spaniards lead very healthy lives. The average life expectancy at birth has reached 76 years for men and 83 years for women, a figure that is higher than average for the industrialized world. Due to a declining birthrate and

To find out more about various Spanish customs (including those of various regional groups), learn some basic Spanish words and get the most up-to-date population figures, visit vgsbooks.com for links.

improvements in the healthcare system, including better prenatal care for expectant mothers, the infant mortality rate—the number of babies who die in the first year of life—has dropped to 4.5 for every 1,000 live births. This rate is lower than the average rate for Western European countries, which is 5 deaths for every 1,000 live births.

Education

Spain's public school system has a long history. Under Moorish rule, the cities of Seville and Granada were important centers of academia. After the Reconquest in the eleventh and twelfth centuries, the Catholic Church's many monasteries and church-run universities became the seats of learning. Advances in education did not occur until the government established a public school system in 1857.

Spain's educational system remained lacking, however. Poor attendance and a lack of resources and supplies kept Spain's education system weak. Improvements were made to the public school system in the 1970s. Since then, the government runs the public school system and allocates funds to public, private, and church-run schools. Regional governments help to oversee their local schools.

Reforms to the system again occurred in 1991, when basic education became mandatory and free for children ages 6 to 16. Primary education, which begins at age 6, lasts for 6 years and is followed by 4 years of secondary education. At age 16, students may choose to take 1- to 2-year vocational training or may take a 2-year university preparation course, called *bachillerato*.

These changes have resulted in a better-educated population. By 2000, 97 percent of Spain's women and 99 percent of Spain's men could read and write. Students must pass the bachillerato to enter a university. Spain has about sixty universities, the largest of which is the University of Madrid, as well as several privately owned universities.

Students hit the books at the University of Madrid library. About 35,000 students enroll at this institution every year.

CULTURAL LIFE

Spain has a rich cultural life, and Spaniards are very proud of their cultural past. Throughout the centuries, Spain has produced world-renowned painters such as El Greco and Pablo Picasso; important literary works such as *El Cid* and *Don Quixote*; musicians such as Plácido Domingo and José Carreras; and dance forms such as the flamenco and bolero. Throughout Spain's colorful and complex history, the Catholic Church has remained a driving force behind the country's cultural life, especially its holidays and festivals.

◉ Holidays and Festivals

Because of the large Catholic majority, many of Spain's holidays are religious in nature. Some of the most important religious holidays include Christmas, Easter, and Epiphany. Semana Santa, or Holy Week, takes place during the week ending with Easter and is one of the most widely celebrated religious events of the year. In virtually every Spanish city and town, processions of people carrying *pasos*—huge,

ornate figures of Catholic saints—march down the streets. Barefoot *penitentes* (penitents, people seeking forgiveness), dressed in floor-length robes with pointed hoods, accompany the procession.

Nonreligious public holidays also occur throughout the year, including New Year's Day on January 1, National Day on October 12, and Constitution Day on December 6. On these days, offices close and people often spend the day with family and friends.

In addition to nationwide events, regions and towns have their own special festivals. During local fiestas, residents honor their town's patron saint. Many of these celebrations include bonfires, games, and amateur bullfights. One of the most popular of these fiestas is San Fermín, which is held each year in Pamplona. The celebration features an exciting event known as the "running of the bulls," when bulls selected for the evening's bullfight are set loose. Hundreds of daring people run through the streets of the city—ahead of the bulls—to the bullring.

Other colorful local holidays include La Tomatina, a tomato-throwing festival in Valencia; the Festes del Merce, a weeklong party in Barcelona during September that honors the city's patroness (Our Lady of Mercy); and Festividad de San Sebastián, or Festival of Saint Sebastian. These events all include music, food, dancing, and fun.

◉ Food

The cuisine of Spain varies from region to region, but some foods are commonplace throughout the country. Rice, fish, seafood, olives, pork, and sausages are mainstays of Spanish meals. Fresh ingredients are important in Spanish cooking, and many shoppers visit the local outdoor *mercado* (market) daily to buy bread, vegetables, fruits, and fish or meat. The ingredients of regional dishes are often grown, raised, or caught locally.

Spaniards typically eat a light breakfast of bread and coffee. *Chocolate con churros*—a thick, rich chocolate drink served with long doughnut-like strips—is also popular. Common midday snacks include the *bocadillo,* a sandwich filled with ham and cheese, or a *tortilla española*—a potato omelet.

Dinner in Spain is served around 2 or 3 P.M. and often consists of three or more courses, including soup, salad, and a main dish. A popular meal is paella, a rice dish prepared with saffron, onions, peppers, and meat or seafood. Fresh bread, water, and wine usually accompany the meal.

A hearty seafood and rice dish, paella is usually prepared in large quantities. Restaurants will offer servings for two or more people.

TORTILLA ESPAÑOLA

This omelet is a favorite snack in Spain. While there are many variations of the recipe, the following is one of the most traditional versions of the dish.

3 eggs

salt to taste

3 tablespoons olive oil

3 large potatoes, peeled and thinly sliced

1 medium onion, peeled and finely chopped

1. In a bowl, beat eggs with fork. Salt to taste.
2. Heat oil in frying pan. Add potato slices and fry for a few minutes.
3. Add onion and mash in with potato. When the mixture browns at the edges, add the eggs. Stir until eggs fully cover the top and bottom of the potato and onion.
4. Fry over low heat. Shake the pan to loosen the omelet and scrape the edges of the pan.
5. When the eggs start to set, place a plate over the pan. Quickly flip the tortilla onto the plate, and then slide the uncooked side back into the pan. Shake the pan gently to keep the omelet from sticking.
6. After about 1 minute, remove from heat and flip onto a plate. (The inside of the omelet should remain slightly runny.) Let set for about 5 minutes before serving. Cut into slices or cubes.

Serves 4

With such a substantial midafternoon meal, Spaniards usually wait until about 9 or 10 P.M. to eat a late supper, which is often made up of lighter foods. Many eateries in Spain serve appetizers called tapas, which are bite-sized portions of calamaries (squid), sausage, hard-boiled egg, or pickled vegetables. For dessert, Spaniards choose fresh fruit or flan, a sweet custard.

Spain is the world's fourth largest producer of wines. Among the most popular types of wine is Rioja, which comes from the valley of the Ebro River. Sherry, another well-known Spanish wine, is produced in Jerez. Sangria (red wine punch) is also popular. Some wineries in Spain specialize in champagnes and brandies.

▶ Literature

Spain has a rich literary tradition. The earliest epic poems described legendary heroes or events. *El Cantar del Mío Cid*, written by an anonymous author in the twelfth century, relates the adventures of El Cid, a soldier during the Reconquest.

Religious writings were some of the earliest and most important elements of Spain's literary history. Saint Teresa of Ávila, one of the first of Spain's women writers, put forth her spiritual teachings in the 1500s in her books *The Way of Perfection* and *The Interior Castle.* Another important author of religious literature was Saint John of the Cross, a contemporary of Saint Teresa. His works include poems, spiritual maxims, and a treatise on theology.

Poetry and novels also found a wide audience during the 1500s and 1600s, Spain's Golden Age for literature. Miguel de Cervantes Saavedra wrote *Don Quixote* in the early 1600s, a popular tale about an old man who believes he is a soldier. Comedies and other types of plays also gained attention during this period. Lope de Vega authored more than one thousand plays, touching on a variety of themes. Tirso de Molina introduced a legendary figure named Don Juan, who would reappear often in later Spanish literature. Pedro Calderón de la Barca, another dramatist, constructed detailed plots on philosophical and religious themes.

> **"At last, having lost his wits completely, he stumbled upon the oddest fancy that ever entered a madman's brain. He believed that it was necessary, both for his own honor and for service of the state, that he should become a knight-errant, roaming through the world with his horse and armor, in quest of adventures and practicing all that had been performed by the knights-errant of whom he had read. "**
>
> —Excerpt from *Don Quixote*

Political and romantic themes showed up in the writings of the 1800s, particularly in the poems of José de Espronceda y Delgado and Gustavo Adolfo Bécquer. The political, social, and religious themes of novelist Benito Pérez Galdós came together in *Dona Perfecta,* a novel about religious intolerance.

Spain's political and economic problems at the end of the 1800s, including its defeat in the Spanish-American War (1898), inspired an influential group of writers known as Generation 98. In their works, these authors reflected on the history and character of Spanish society. Pío Baroja, Antonio Buero Vallejo, José Ortega y Gasset, and Federico García Lorca became the best known authors of the period.

During the Spanish civil war, many writers and scholars were considered a threat to the new regime. Many fled or were killed or exiled.

As a result, Spanish literature developed outside of Spain. The Nobel Prize winner Camilo José Cela wrote *The Family of Pascual Duarte* in 1961, while living elsewhere in Europe.

Under Franco, literature was censored, especially political works. After Franco's death in 1975, writers once again were free to write without constraints. Modern Spanish writers use a variety of literary forms—novels, plays, poems, essays, and short stories—to discuss themes ranging from history to health and fitness. Authors such as Julian Rios, who wrote *Loves That Bind,* and Nuria Barrios, author of *El Zoo Sentimental,* are gaining worldwide recognition for their works. Important contemporary women writers include novelists Adelaida Garcia Morales and Ana Maria Matute.

▶ Music and Dance

Throughout Spain's history, local musical traditions have been passed down from generation to generation. The tunes and rhythms of traditional folk songs appear in the *sardana* from Catalonia, the *jota* from Aragón, the Gypsy flamenco, the bolero, the fandango, and many other forms of music and dance.

Spanish folk music influenced the works of many early composers. During the reign of Ferdinand and Isabella, Antonio de Cabezón and

Female flamenco dancers often wear brightly colored dresses adorned with ruffles. Spanish Gypsies drew on various traditions to create both flamenco and the accompanying music, *cante jondo*, a hypnotic, wailing vocal style paired with guitar.

Juan del Encina wrote popular piano music and lyrics. Musicians began using the organ and the six-string *vihuela*, or Spanish guitar, in the sixteenth century. By the 1600s, dramatists and composers were working together on Spain's first operas and *zarzuelas*—musical plays with songs, dances, and spoken passages.

Vihuela player

Classical composers in the 1800s also relied on folk traditions. Joaquín Turina wrote the *Seville Symphony*, and Isaac Albéniz gained fame for *Iberia*, a suite of piano works. In the twentieth century, Joaquín Rodrigo became one of Spain's leading classical composers.

During the 1920s, musician Andrés Segovia generated renewed interest in the traditional Spanish guitar. Many composers began writing guitar music, and the instrument's popularity spread to other parts of Europe and to Latin America. Other well known Spanish guitarists include Narciso Yepes and Regino Sainz. Spain's other most famous instrumentalists of the twentieth century include pianist Alicia de Larrocha and the late cellist Pablo Casals. Considered one of the best cellists of all time, Casals also composed and conducted.

Spaniards listen to the classical music performances of the National Orchestra and of the Camerata in Madrid. Opera is also popular in Spain, which is home to well known opera singers Plácido Domingo, José Carreras, and Montserrat Caballé.

Some contemporary Spanish musicians combine the country's musical traditions to make new sounds. For example, groups such as Ketama fuse flamenco and rock to create a sound called Gypsy rock. Radio Tarifa is popular for combining flamenco with North African and medieval music. Balladeer Julio Iglesias gained fame in concert appearances around the world for his blend of Latin sounds and pop, and his son Enrique Iglesias has become a popular international pop star.

Pop star and heartthrob Enrique Iglesias helped bring Spanish-language pop into the international musical mainstream.

Spanish musical elements are also evident in the songs of Central and Latin America, as well as the Caribbean. Spanish colonists brought their music and instruments with them to these early settlements, and soon Spanish instruments were blended with Latin American songs. Spain's musical heritage is still an important part of the music of these countries, and over the years, these unique sounds have combined with American pop and African rhythms to create an entirely new genre or music called Latin pop.

Film

The earliest Spanish film was *Ría en un Café,* directed by Fructuos Gelabert in 1897. Early directors such as Segundo de Chomón and Luis Buñuel produced brilliant and original works that gained worldwide attention in the early 1900s.

Spain's film industry fell under heavy censorship during Franco's rule, and few original works emerged from Spanish filmmakers at this time. In the late 1970s, government supervision of the industry relaxed, allowing directors such as Carlos Saura to once again create innovative pieces.

After Franco's death, the government eliminated its censorship laws. Unfortunately for Spanish filmmakers, many audiences preferred foreign films, which had long been forbidden, over those produced by their fellow Spaniards. Nevertheless, many Spanish directors became famous overseas for their works.

Spanish directors are becoming a powerful force in the world film industry. One of the first to gain worldwide recognition was Pedro Almodóvar. In 1986 Almodóvar directed the then up-and-coming

Film director Pedro Almodóvar won an Academy Award in the category of Best Foreign Film for *All about My Mother* in 2000.

Spanish actor Antonio Banderas in *La Ley del Deseo* (*Law of Desire*). Fernando Trueba won an Academy Award for Best Foreign Film with his *Belle Epoque* (*The Age of Beauty*) in 1993. Alejandro Amenabar gained international attention with his 1997 suspense film *Abre los Ojos* (*Open Your Eyes*). In 2001 Amenabar directed the American thriller *The Others*. Another important filmmaker is José Luis Cerda, who directed *La Lengua de las Mariposas* (*Butterfly*) in 2000.

◉ Fine Arts

The earliest known art forms in Spain were the cave paintings in Altamira. Since then, Spain has produced some of the world's most famous and influential painters.

During the Middle Ages, paintings by unknown artists adorned the walls of public buildings, particularly churches. In the 1300s, individual artists began receiving public credit for their works. One of the earliest Spanish masters was painter Ferrer Bassa.

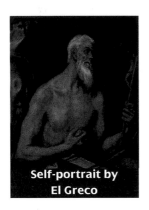

Self-portrait by El Greco

One of Spain's most famous early painters, Domenikos Theotokopoulos (1541–1614), is better known as El Greco (The Greek). As a young man, El Greco moved from his homeland of Greece to Toledo, where he spent his life painting portraits featuring elongated figures, mystical religious scenes, and landscapes with contrasting colors and dark shadows.

Another important artist, Diego Velázquez (1599–1660), painted religious works and royal portraits. *Las Meninas*, probably Velázquez's most famous painting, is a masterpiece in its use of color, light, shadow, and space.

Francisco de Goya y Lucientes (1746–1828), a painter in the royal court, produced frescoes, tapestries, and engravings. Goya's command of mood and technique made him a leading figure in nineteenth-century European art.

Modern Spanish painters were greatly influenced by the art scene in Paris, France. In the early twentieth century, artists Pablo Picasso and Juan Grís both moved to Paris, where they developed a new style known as Cubism. Cubist painters abandoned realism for an abstract art form that emphasized geometric shapes and that rearranged objects in new relationships.

Grís later developed synthetic cubism, a collage technique that added fabric, cardboard, newsprint, and other materials to the painted canvas. Picasso's early paintings ranged from realistic portraits to scenes in somber tones of blue and rose. His later works adopted surrealism—a dreamlike art form full of complex symbols.

Go to vgsbooks.com! Click on the various links where you'll be connected to Spain's rich cultural heritage: artwork, recipes, holidays and festivals, literature, and more.

Joan Miró also became a leader in surrealism. Miró's lively abstract paintings mixed bright colors and startling shapes. Salvador Dalí created outrageous and flamboyant surrealist paintings that attracted worldwide attention.

Contemporary Spanish artists continue to make international names for themselves through their thought-provoking works. These include painter Antoni Tápies, who paints with a variety of materials to give his works an unusual feel, and sculptor Juan Muñoz, whose works are characterized by human figures arranged in detailed architectural settings.

Architecture

Spain's long and varied history has left the country with a wealth of architectural styles. Ancient Roman aqueducts still stand in cities such as Segovia and Tarragona, and eighth-century Islamic mosques survive in Andalusia. The Alhambra, a Moorish palace built in the fourteenth century, dominates the cityscape of Granada. Sixteenth-century cathedrals

The most famous building in Granada is the Alhambra. The name *Alhambra* comes from an Arabic root that means "red castle."

dot the entire peninsula, and modern skyscrapers rise from urban centers. Sections of ancient stone walls, bridges, and gates can still be found in old cities like Toledo and Ávila. Most towns have bullrings and central plazas, or squares, where people stroll and gather to chat. In central Spain, castles loom nearly everywhere. In fact, more than 1,400 historical castles and palaces still stand.

The strong colors, shapes, and images that characterized the works of Spanish cubist and surrealist painters also are found in the architecture of Antoní Gaudí (1852–1926). This modern Catalán architect designed buildings that grab the attention with their strange patterns and unique details. At Güell Park in Barcelona, Gaudí's techniques imitate natural forms such as trees and flowing water. Gaudí's unfinished masterpiece, the Sagrada Familia (Holy Family) in Barcelona, is a looming four-towered cathedral that shows strong influences of more ancient building styles. One of the most exciting buildings in Spain is the eye-catching Guggenheim Museum Bilbao in that same city. Designed by modern U.S. architect Frank Gehry, the museum features a combination of interconnecting

Although Gaudí created extensive plans for the Sagrada Familia, he died before its completion. In fact, the cathedral has remained under construction since 1883 and is not expected to be finished until 2050.

shapes and glass walls. World-renowned Spanish architect Santiago Calatrava designed the Tenerife Opera House, a dazzlingly white modern building located in Tenerife's capital city in the Canary Islands.

Guggenheim Bilbao

Sports and Recreation

Soccer—called *fútbol* in Spain—is the nation's favorite sport, and almost every city and town has a team. The biggest rivals, however, are the nation's popular world-class professional teams—Real Madrid and F. C. Barcelona. Spain has produced a number of international soccer stars.

Besides soccer, Spaniards enjoy basketball, cycling, tennis, skiing, swimming, and sailing. *Pelota* (also called jai alai), an intense game that originated in Basque Country, involves two players who use a basketlike racket to fling a small, hard ball against a wall. Spain has produced world-famous athletes such as tennis player Arantxa Sanchez Vicario, cyclist Pedro Delgado, and golfer Severiano Ballesteros.

The sport of bullfighting, a traditional part of Spanish culture, remains popular. The three-part bullfight is a theatrical production that begins with the entrance into the ring of the matadors and their assistants, the picadors and the banderilleros. The picador circles the bullring on horseback and jabs the bull with a sharp lance to tire it. Next, the banderilleros stab the bull with long darts.

The matador finally enters the ring and lures the bull into charging toward an outstretched red cape. After the wounded bull is exhausted, the matador finishes by killing the bull with a long sword. The strength, endurance, bravery, and grace of both the matador and the bull attract bullfighting fans—not the chance to see a bull die. Some of the most important contemporary matadors include El Cordobes and Manolete.

Bullfighting has been important to Spanish culture for centuries. The first historic bullfight took place in 1158 to honor the coronation of King Alfonso VIII.

THE ECONOMY

Until the mid-1900s, Spain's economy was agrarian, meaning it relied on agriculture. During Franco's regime in the 1950s and 1960s, the country began to modernize, making manufacturing and industry the heart of its economic base. In the 1970s, Spain attracted foreign investment, which helped the nation's economy further expand and modernize. Business loans encouraged manufacturing and spurred international trade. The financial and service sectors, which include banking and tourism, also grew in importance. Spain suddenly had a more prosperous and stable economy than it had ever known.

In 1986 Spain secured membership in what eventually became the European Union (EU). The members of this international trade alliance have removed trade barriers among member nations. EU nations together produce a huge volume of goods and make up one of the world's largest single markets for products and services. This has led to economic growth and has brought prosperity to many Spaniards.

Although industry, trade, and services have flourished, some of Spain's citizens have not benefited from this growth. Farmers find themselves unable to make a living, forcing them to leave their land to find new employment. This, in turn, has led to crowded conditions and wide-spread unemployment in some cities.

Despite an economic upturn at the end of the twentieth century, Spain still faced the challenges of high prices, increasing inflation rates, and rising unemployment. In 1994 an estimated 22 percent of the workforce did not have jobs. Between 1996 and 2000, the creation of new jobs, particularly in high-tech industries and the service sector, helped reduce this number to 9 percent.

The service sector, which provides services rather than producing goods, accounts for about 65 percent of Spain's gross domestic product (GDP) and employs 64 percent of the labor force. The GDP is the value of all goods and services produced by the country in a year. The government employs many service workers in hospitals, in schools, and in administrative offices. Service workers in the private sector hold jobs in banking, tourism, and transportation.

Trade and Tourism

Spain's main trading partners are other EU countries and the United States. Exports include citrus fruits, wines, fish products, olive oil, textiles, cars, and ships. Petroleum, raw cotton, cereals, meat products, vegetable oils, chemicals, and heavy machinery are the major imports. Because of its limited natural resources, Spain has a trade deficit, spending more on imports than it earns from exports. The income from Spain's tourist industry helps to alleviate this deficit.

Spain's thriving tourism industry attracts more than 50 million vacationers each year, bringing about $25 billion into the country. Foreign visitors use hotel and restaurant services, buy Spanish-made goods, and eat locally grown foods. Tourist spending raises Spain's income, thereby reducing the nation's trade deficit, and creates jobs. Like most countries, Spain's tourist industry experienced a decline after the September 11, 2001, terrorist attacks on the United States. But by the end of 2002, the industry had rebounded and even recorded some growth. One reason may be that Europeans still consider Spain a safe destination during times of international discord. And many European travelers who had planned trips to the United States or overseas instead opted for Spain as their vacation spot.

Major tourist centers in Spain include Madrid, the Balearic Islands, and the coastal areas. The Costa Brava, near Barcelona, attracts many

Tourists flock to Spain's many beaches, including this one in Majorca.

sun-seeking vacationers, as do the Costa del Sol and the Costa Blanca in the south. Many history buffs also visit the ornate castles, palaces, and cathedrals scattered throughout the country.

Spain has also become a favorite destination for business travelers. Several cities have modern facilities for large trade fairs and business conventions. Recreational areas have been developed to attract visitors. Ski resorts in the Pyrenees, the Cantabrians, and other ranges, for example, draw many winter sports enthusiasts.

More than one hundred golf courses are scattered across Spain, mostly on the Mediterranean coast and on the islands. Many of the courses are internationally known and sponsor prestigious professional tournaments year-round.

But tourism has its costs. Large crowds of people mean more garbage on the beaches, more cars on the road, and the building of more hotels—all of which damage the natural beauty that the tourists come to see. In 2001 several tourist areas, including the Balearic Islands, started an environmental tourist tax. This was included in the cost of hotels. The money from this additional tax will go to conservation efforts to help protect the environment and to repair the damage brought on by the heavy influx of tourists each year.

Manufacturing

In the 1950s and 1960s, Spain became more industrialized. No longer entirely dependent on agriculture, industry became the backbone of Spain's economy. Manufacturing continues to be a central part of Spain's economy. Along with construction and mining, the sector employs about 29 percent of the jobholders and produces 31 percent of the GDP. While the government operates certain industries, particularly the country's steel mills, most factories are owned by private businesses.

The automobile industry, one of Spain's most important manufacturing sectors, produces cars for sale in Spain and for export. Automobile factories are located in Barcelona, Madrid, Saragossa, Valencia, and Valladolid. The country's car-producing factories rank among the world's most efficient, producing more motor parts per hour than the auto industries of other car-producing nations. Ford and General Motors have plants in Spain. The country remains one of the world's largest exporters of passenger cars.

Bilbao, Madrid, and Barcelona are the country's leading industrial centers. Shipbuilding remains important in the north, where state-owned factories produce steel for many of the nation's heavy industries. In Barcelona, textiles and shoes are major products. Spanish workers also manufacture chemicals, footwear, and foodstuffs. Spain is also investing in new industries, such as information technology and telecommunications equipment to further boost the manufacturing sector. Foreign investment has helped to develop these new and important parts of Spain's economy.

Agriculture

Spain's poor soil and sparse rainfall make farming difficult. Yet almost all available land is used for agriculture. Although the majority of Spain's farmers own their land, about one-third of the workers are employed by large-scale landowners. In fact, a very small number of landowners hold half of Spain's farmland. The largest tracts lie in Andalusia in southern Spain. Most small farms are located in the northern half of the country.

About 7 percent of the nation's workers farm or fish for a living. Farmers and fishers contribute about 4 percent of Spain's GDP. The most important crops include barley, wheat, citrus fruits, olives, wine grapes, and rice. The raising of livestock—mostly sheep, goats, and cattle—is also a key part of the farming sector. Grain crops and pasture for sheep and goats are common in the north, while citrus trees, olive groves, and vineyards thrive in the south and along the eastern coast.

A group of Galician fishers prepare for the day's work. Fish and seafood are vital to Spanish cuisine, and both sell well domestically and abroad.

Vineyards dot the Spanish landscape. The nation has fifty recognized wine regions and produces nearly 100,000 gallons (378,540 liters) of wine each year.

Spain leads the world in the production of olive oil, and the nation is among the world's top producers of wines.

Spain's fishing fleet—one of the largest in the world—hauls in a total of more than 1 million tons (900,000 metric tons) of anchovies, sardines, hake, cod, tuna, squid, and octopus each year. Crustaceans and mollusks are also important. The main fishing ports lie along the Atlantic Ocean and in the Bay of Biscay. However, overfishing and water pollution have deleted fish populations off Spain's coasts, resulting in dwindling catches in recent years.

Transportation and Energy

Spain's transportation system includes roads, railways, airports, and ports. The nation's highways line the coasts and link major cities in Spain with Madrid. Most routes are in fairly good condition, serving tourists, commuting Spaniards, and truck drivers. In addition, most families own their own vehicles. Nearly 413,000 miles (664,000 km) of roads cross the country, including 6,412 miles (10,317 km) of motorway and almost 15,000 miles (24,140 km) of main roads. Lesser-used roadways are often unpaved.

Spain's railroad network sustained heavy damage during the civil war of the 1930s, and later repairs did little to improve the system. A plan for modernization began in the 1960s and produced the high-speed trains that link Madrid with Barcelona and with Seville. Nevertheless, the state-owned railroads in Spain still have narrower tracks than those of northern Europe. As a result, train travelers must stop at the French border and change trains. In 2000 the government

Passengers wait to board a train in Madrid's main railway station.

announced plans to privatize the rail system by 2004, allowing private operators to own and run the state railways. And in 2001, Spain and Portugal agreed to a high-speed train route to link the two countries by 2008. Another proposed plan would link France to Catalonia.

Spain has forty-two airports, with more than half of them equipped to handle international flights. Major airports in Madrid, Barcelona, Málaga, Palma de Mallorca, Seville, Valencia, and Las Palma handle most international air traffic. Construction of an airport in Ciudad Real was announced in 2001, with completion scheduled for 2004. Iberia Airlines, Spain's largest state-owned airline, employs thousands of people and flies to major cities around the world. In 1999 Iberia underwent the first stage of privatization before the second phase was postponed indefinitely. Other major airlines are Air Europa and Spanair. Smaller private airlines make trips to other European destinations and to regional airports within Spain.

Spain's long coasts have a large number of port cities. Most of the principal ports accommodate both passenger carriers and freight ships. Numerous smaller ports specialize in regional trade and commuter ferry traffic. Transmediterranea—the state-owned shipping company—links the Spanish mainland to the Balearics, the Canaries, and northern Africa with year-round daily service.

Spain relies on foreign countries for much of its energy sources. Mining is not a large industry, and less than 1 percent of the labor force works in mining. Existing mining operations extract iron ore in the north, near the factories that produce iron and steel. Mercury, lead, zinc, copper, small amounts of natural gas and oil, and poor-quality coal also are mined. Spain remains dependent on foreign oil, with Mexico as its largest supplier. Hydroelectric power supplies Spain with about one-fifth of the energy it consumes, and nuclear power provides about 30 percent of Spain's energy.

Visit vgsbooks.com for up-to-date information about Spain's economy and a link to the current exchange rate where you can convert U.S. dollars to euros.

The Future

Spain and its people underwent important political and economic changes in the latter half of the twentieth century, giving the country an entirely new flavor. Politically, the young democratic government, while facing many obstacles, has thus far proven stable.

However, party divisions and international politics, particularly Prime Minister Aznar's support of the U.S.-led war in Iraq, have left people highly critical of the current administration. And issues related to national identity continue to plague the country. Many ethnic groups continue to demand self-rule, and the development of strong regional governments means a weaker national government. These political problems must be solved before Spain can fully realize its potential.

Economically, Spain has rapidly developed from an agrarian society to a modern industrial nation. This new economy has experienced several extreme ups and downs, though it seems to be growing steadily. In 2002 Spain and other members of the EU agreed to replace their national currencies with the euro, which became common currency for all participating countries. This transition was intended to help the member countries strengthen their common economies and unite their resources.

The euro seems to be helping Spain in several ways. Before the switch, Spaniards fearing stricter tax laws with the new currency spent more pesetas (Spain's former currency) on consumer goods and luxury items, stimulating the economy. After adopting the euro, Spain and other member countries could invest their money in euro-based economies without worrying about exchange rates among these economies. Time will tell how much affect the euro will truly have on Spain's economy.

While Spaniards have made huge strides to modernize their nation, the transition to a new economic and political system will continue to take time and effort. But the people of Spain are determined to address these issues and to once again make their country a strong nation.

Timeline

CA. 200,000 B.C.	Humans settle on the Iberian Peninsula.
CA. 25,000 B.C.	Residents of the Iberian Peninsula create cave paintings.
CA. 1000 B.C.	Phoenician traders set up colonies at Cádiz and Málaga.
CA. 900 B.C.	Celts move into the area.
237 B.C.	Carthaginian forces land on the Iberian Peninsula.
206 B.C.	Roman forces defeat Carthage, adding Iberia to their empire. They dub the area Hispania.
A.D. 401	Germanic peoples invade Spain, reducing Roman rule.
711	The Moors begin invading Spain, bringing Islam with them.
1248	Christians control the peninsula, except for the Moorish city of Granada.
1348-1351	The Black Death spreads throughout Spain, killing almost one-third of the population.
1478	The Spanish Inquisition begins.
1479	The kingdoms of Castilla y León and Aragón are united through marriage.
1492	Christian forces capture Granada, forcing Jews and Muslims to convert or leave. Christopher Columbus claims the West Indies for Spain.
1516	Charles I (also Charles V) becomes king of Spain, the start of Habsburg rule in Spain.
1701-1714	The Habsburg and Bourbon dynasties fight the War of Spanish Succession.
1808	French emperor Napoleon Bonaparte invades Spain and places his brother Joseph on the Spanish throne.
1813	Spanish forces drive French rulers from Spain.
1834	The Inquisition is officially abolished.
1898	Spain fights the United States in the Spanish-American War. Spain is forced to turn over Puerto Rico, the Philippine Islands, and Guam, as well as temporary control of Cuba, to the United States.
1923	General Miguel Primo de Rivera takes control of Spain.
1930	General Primo de Rivera is forced to resign.
1936	General Francisco Franco and supporters launch a military campaign to overthrow Spain's existing government. Civil war starts.

1939   Franco becomes dictator.

1953   Franco allows the United States to establish military bases in Spain in exchange for financial aid.

1959   The Basque terrorist organization ETA is founded.

1975   Franco dies. Juan Carlos becomes king.

1977   Spain grants limited self-rule to Basque Country and Catalonia.

1982   Spain joins NATO.

1986   Spain joins the European Economic Community, which later becomes the European Union.

1992   Barcelona hosts the Summer Olympics. Madrid is named the "Cultural Capital of Europe."

1998   ETA announces a cease-fire and attempts negotiations with the Spanish government.

1999   The ETA cease-fire ends.

2002   Spain replaces the peseta with the euro as its new currency.

2003   Prime Minister Aznar agrees to support the United States in its war against Iraq, despite widespread opposition among Spaniards.

COUNTRY NAME Kingdom of Spain

AREA 195,363 square miles (505,988 sq. km)

MAIN LANDFORMS Cantabrian Mountains, Coastal Plain, the Meseta, Pyrenees Mountains, Sierra de Guadarrama, Sierra Morena, Sierra Nevada

HIGHEST POINT Pico de Teide, 12,198 feet (3,718 m) above sea level

LOWEST POINT Sea level

MAJOR RIVERS Duero, Ebro, Guadalquivir, Guadiana, Tajo

ANIMALS brown bears, chamois, foxes, lynx, martens, mountain goats, weasels, wild boars, wolves

CAPITAL CITY Madrid

OTHER MAJOR CITIES Barcelona, Bilbao, Saragossa, Seville, Valencia

OFFICIAL LANGUAGE Spanish

MONETARY UNIT Euro. (100 cents=1 euro)

SPANISH CURRENCY

Since 2002 Spain's monetary unit has been the euro. Spain's former currency, the peseta, was as steeped in history as the country itself. The peseta was derived from *pesos de ocho,* or pieces of eight, a unit of money established in the late fifteenth century. These silver coins arose from the discovery of silver in Spain's colonies in South America. By the mid-1500s, the Spaniards had established a mint in Mexico to create the coins. As the Spanish Empire declined in the 1800s, so did the peso. In 1868 the peseta emerged as a replacement for the weakened peso. The peseta served as the Spanish currency until January 1, 2002, when Spain was one of eleven European countries that switched to the euro. This move was designed to link the countries economically and strengthen the member countries' currency.

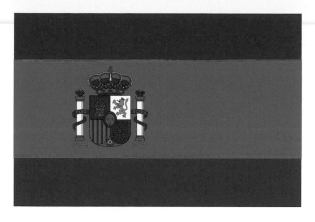

Spain's current flag was adopted in 1981. It features three horizontal bands of color. The top and bottom bands are red, and the middle band—which is twice as thick as the surrounding bands—is yellow. The national coat of arms sits on the left side of the yellow band. The coat of arms is the royal seal framed by two pillars. The symbols on the shield represent the historic kingdoms of Spain.

Spain's national anthem is the "Marcha Real," or "Royal March." While its origins are unknown, the music for the anthem was discovered in 1761 in an infantry book describing regulation bugle calls. In 1770 King Carlos III declared the tune an honor march, making it a traditional part of official public events. The tune soon became the unofficial Spanish anthem, and Spaniards dubbed it the "Royal March," since it was always played at events in the presence of Spanish royalty. From 1931 to 1939, "Marcha Real" was replaced by another anthem. After Franco assumed power, however, "Marcha Real" once again resumed its status.

The anthem has no official lyrics.

For a link where you can listen to Spain's national anthem, "Marcha Real," go to vgsbooks.com.

Flag · **National Anthem**

RAUL GONZÁLEZ BLANCO (b. 1977) Raul González Blanco is a soccer player for the team Real Madrid. Blanco started playing for the Real in 1994, and he made his professional debut in 1996 at the age of 19. Since starting his professional career, Blanco has helped his team win the Spanish League championship in 1995, 1997, and 2001. In 2002 he finished as the season's top scorer. Blanco was born in Madrid.

SANTIAGO CALATRAVA (b. 1951) Born in Benimamet, Calatrava is a progressive modern architect. After studying architecture in Valencia and civil engineering in Zurich, he began to enter his work in competitions in hopes of securing commissions. His plan worked, and throughout the 1980s and 1990s he designed a series of bridges for locations throughout Spain. More recent works include the Sondica Airport in Bilbao, the Tenerife Opera House in the Canary Islands, and a redesign of the Milwaukee Art Museum in Wisconsin.

PLÁCIDO DOMINGO (b. 1941) Born in Madrid, Plácido Domingo has earned the title the King of Opera. He made his debut with the Metropolitan Opera in 1968 and has since appeared in more than four hundred performances there. He appears in performances throughout the world and has received many awards for his conducting and performances.

FRANCISCO FRANCO (1892–1975) General Francisco Franco was born in El Ferrol. He joined the army in 1910 and quickly earned a reputation for efficiency and dedication. In the 1920s, Franco's role in suppressing revolts in Morocco made him a national hero, and he was made army chief of staff in 1935. The following year, Franco took part in a revolt against the Spanish government, a move that plunged the country into civil war. By 1939 Franco and his supporters had seized control, with a heavy loss in life and much destruction. He reigned as dictator until his death in 1975.

ANTONÍ GAUDÍ (1852–1926) Antoní Gaudí was one of Spain's most famous architects. Gaudí gained worldwide fame through his unique blend of traditional and creative elements. Born in Reus, he attended school in Barcelona, where he studied classical and modern architectural designs. Gaudí's most important works include the public buildings Casa Calvet, for which he won an award, and La Pedrera. His masterpiece is the Sagrada Familia cathedral, which has become one of Barcelona's most important monuments.

ENRIQUE IGLESIAS (b. 1975) Enrique Iglesias is the son of Spain's most famous singer, Julio Iglesias (b. 1943). Born in Madrid, Enrique Iglesias spent much of his youth living in Miami, Florida. In 1995 Iglesias released his first album, *Enrique Iglesias*, a Latin pop blend that soon made him a superstar in the Spanish-speaking world. His second album, *Vivir*, earned a Grammy Award and made him an international star. His most recent work is his 2002 album *Quizás*.

ISABELLA I (1451–1504) Isabella I became queen of Castilla y Léon in 1479, after the death of her half brother Henry IV. Isabella's marriage to Ferdinand of Portugal in 1469 united the kingdoms of Castile and Aragón, as Ferdinand had become king of Aragón. Isabella and Ferdinand made many improvements and increased their power. But they also instituted the Inquisition, to weed out nonbelievers in the Catholic faith. Queen Isabella sponsored Christopher Columbus's voyage to the Americas, established schools, and supported the arts. Isabella was born in Castilla y Léon.

ALICIA DE LARROCHA (b. 1923) Alicia de Larrocha is considered the world's greatest Spanish pianist. Her first public appearance took place in 1929, at the age of 6. She is internationally known for her performances of Spanish and classical music, and her performances often include the music of famous Spanish composers, such as Isaac Albéniz. Her works have earned her numerous awards, including four Grammy awards, two Records of the Year, and international honors for her contribution to the fine arts. In 2002 de Larrocha ended her performing career with a concert at Carnegie Hall in New York City. She was born in Barcelona.

PABLO PICASSO (1881–1973) Born in Málaga, Pablo Picasso was one of the most important painters and sculptors in twentieth-century art. Around 1907, Picasso helped create a revolutionary new painting genre called cubism, which depicts objects from multiple points of view at the same time. His most important works include *Les Demoiselles d'Avignon*, *The Three Musicians*, and *Guernica*.

TERESA OF ÁVILA (1515-1582) Saint Teresa of Ávila was one of the earliest and most important of Spain's religious writers. In 1535 she entered a convent at Ávila, where she became a nun. In the 1560s and 1570s, Saint Teresa opened several convents and served as head of a monastery in Ávila. Her writings include her autobiography as well as two important spiritual teachings, *The Way of Perfection* and *The Interior Castle*. For her accomplishments, she was canonized (elevated to sainthood) in 1622.

ARANTXA SANCHEZ VICARIO (b. 1971) Arantxa Sanchez Vicario is a professional women's tennis player. Vicario started playing tennis at the age of four by following her brothers to the court when they played. She made her professional debut in 1985. Since then, she has won thirteen Grand Slam titles. Vicario has used her fame to establish the Foundation Sanchez Vicario in 1998 to raise money for children in Spain who cannot afford to pursue a career in sports. She also raises money for terminally ill children. She was born in Barcelona.

BALEARIC ISLANDS The Balearic Islands are a huge draw for both international and local tourists. The islands boast fine beaches and an abundance of sunshine. In addition, they have retained many of their historical elements, such as Gothic churches, Stone Age ruins, and small villages.

BARCELONA Barcelona's highlights include unique architecture, museums, and historical sights. The architecture of Antoní Gaudí can be found in the Sagrada Familia Cathedral and the Güell Park. Museums include the Museo Picasso and the Fundacio Joan Miró, two modern art museums that display the works of two Spanish masters. The city also boasts an impressive Gothic cathedral, which is also the site of Sunday afternoon performances by Catalán dancers. The City History Museum is a unique museum that features a subterranean walk through excavated portions of the Roman and Visigothic cities. Barcelona also boasts some of the best marketplaces in Spain.

GRANADA The city of Granada, once the finest Islamic city on the Iberian Peninsula, retains much of its Islamic architecture. The most impressive attraction here is the Alhambra, considered one of the greatest examples of Islamic architecture. The Alhambra includes a fortress, palace, and gardens—all of which are famous for their great beauty and elaborate details. Other highlights include an Archaeological Museum, Arab Baths, Ferdinand and Isabella's burial sites, and a sixteenth-century cathedral.

MADRID Spain's capital city has many interesting sights, including museums, galleries, parks, and monuments. The Museo del Prado is considered one of the most spectacular art museums in the world, featuring works from Spanish, Flemish, and Italian artists from the fifteenth to the nineteenth centuries. Other popular sights are the Palacio Real, or the Royal Palace, which has elaborate wall and ceiling decorations, the Catedral de Nuestra Senora de la Almudena, a cathedral that was under construction for more than 100 years, and the Real Jardin Botanico, or Royal Botanical Gardens. In addition, Madrid is home to Plaza de Toros Monumental de las Ventas, the world's largest bullring.

TOLEDO Toledo is actually an intact medieval city with many churches, Moorish castles, and other historical monuments. Some of the highlights in this fascinating city include a cathedral with murals and works by such Spanish masters as El Greco, Velázquez, and Goya. In addition, archaeologists have recently uncovered a fourth-century Roman basilica, the oldest in Spain.

Arabic: the language of the historic Moors; the modern language spoken across much of southwest Asia and northern Africa

Black Death: a type of bubonic plague that spread through Europe in the 1300s, killing hundreds of thousands of people

Catholicism: a Christian religion based on the teachings of Jesus Christ and founded in the first century A.D. The pope, who is based in Vatican City in Italy, is the head of the Catholic Church.

coup d'état: a sudden and decisive political action, with or without force, that usually results in a change of government

European Union: an organization of European countries that promotes cooperation among its members in matters of politics and economics

gross domestic product (GDP): a measure of the total vaule of goods and services produced within a country in a cetrain amount of time (usually one year). A similar measurement is gross national product (GNP). GDP and GNP are often measured in terms of purchasing power parity (PPP). PPP converts values to international dollars, making it possible to compare how much similar goods and service cost to the residents of different countries.

Islam: a religion based on the Prophet Muhammad's teaching and founded in the seventh century A.D. Islam's holy book is the Quran, which, among other things, describes five fundamental religious duties (or pillars) for its followers.

Moors: Muslim groups from northern Africa who conquered Spain in the sixth century and ruled for nearly six hundred years

mosque: an Islamic place of worship

Mozarabs: a Christian living in Moorish Spain

Muslim: a follower of Islam

nationalist: a person who feels supreme loyalty toward his or her nation and places a primary emphasis on the promotion of a national culture and national interests

Protestantism: Western Christian religions not affiliated with the Catholic Church; Protestants do not recognize the universal authority of the pope

Reconquest: Christian efforts, beginning in the eighth century, to retake Moorish lands in Spain

serfdom: a system in which peasants, or serfs, are required to render services to their lord, often in exchange for land or protection

All About Spain. N.d.
Website: <http://www.red2000.com/spain/culture-index.html> (January 13, 2002).
This website features information about Spanish culture and popular customs, including flamenco, bullfighting, fiestas, and foods.

Background Notes. June 2002
Website: <http://www.state.gov/r/pa/ei/bgn/> (January 13, 2002)
This site is run by the U.S. Department of State and provides information about Spain and other foreign countries, including the political conditions, foreign relations, and economy.

Christian, Rebecca. *Cooking the Spanish Way.* Minneapolis: Lerner Publications Company, 2001.
This cookbook features recipes from Spain, as well as an introduction to the land and culture. Holidays and festivals are also discussed.

CountryWatch. January 2003
Website: <http://www.countrywatch.com/> (January 12, 2003)
CountryWatch has information about Spain, including political history, economic conditions, environmental issues, and social customs.

Ellingham, Mark, and John Fisher. *The Rough Guide to Spain.* London: Rough Guides, 2001.
This travel guide covers sights to see in Spain, as well as giving a brief history of the land and the people.

Europa Year World Book. Vol. 2. London: Europa Publications Ltd., 2001.
The article covering Spain includes recent events, vital statistics, and economic information.

Grabowski, John. *Spain.* San Diego: Lucent Books, 2000.
This book offers an excellent overview of Spain's history, geography, and culture. Grabowski also discusses the country's current issues and the challenges it will face in the near future.

Lonely Planet World Guide: Destination Spain. N.d.
Website: <http://www.lonelyplanet.com/destinations/europe/spain> (January 13, 2003)
The bureau offers Spain's current population figures, vital statistics, land area, and more. Special articles cover the latest environmental and health issues that concern Spain and other featured nations.

Miller, Arthur. *Spain.* Philadelphia: Chelsea House, 1999.
This book discusses the history, geography, and people of Spain.

Population Reference Bureau. January 2003
Website: <http://www.prb.org> (January 12, 2003)
The bureau offers Spain's current population figures, vital statistics, land area, and more. Special articles cover the latest environmental and health issues that concern Spain and other featured nations.

Simonis, Damien, et al. *Spain.* **Footscray, Australia: Lonely Planet, 2001.**

In addition to the sights to see, this travel guide includes an excellent section on the culture of Spain.

Statesman's Yearbook. **London: Macmillan, 2001.**

This resource features information about Spain's historical events, industry and trade, climate and topography, as well as suggestions for further reading.

Williams, Mark. *The Story of Spain.* **Fuengirola, Spain: Santana Books, 2000.**

Williams gives a comprehensive history of Spain, from prehistoric times to the mid-1990s. In addition to Spanish history, each chapter offers a list of important sites relating to the historic period.

The World Factbook. **January 1, 2002**
Website: <http://www.cia.gov/cia/publications/factbook.html> (January 15, 2003)

This website features up-to-date information about the people, land, economy, and government of Spain. International issues are also briefly covered.

Anderson, Robert. *Salvador Dali.* **New York: Franklin Watts, 2002.**
This biography covers the life of one of Spain's greatest modern artists.

Anderson, Wayne. *The ETA: Spain's Basque Terrorists.* **New York: Rosen Publishing Group, 2003.**
Anderson discusses the foundation of this terrorist group as well as its aims.

Cervantes, Miguel de. *Don Quixote.* **Translated and abridged by Joanne Fink. Parsippany, NJ: Silver Burdett Press, 1984.**
Fink has adapted Cervantes' classic tale into a kid-friendly version to tell the story of the man of La Mancha. Many publishers offer translated editions of the unabridged text as well.

Day, Nancy. *Your Travel Guide to Renaissance Europe.* **Minneapolis: Runestone Press, 2001.**
Learn about the effects of the Black Death and life in the court of Ferdinand and Isabella.

Finkelstein, Norman. *The Other 1492: Jewish Settlement in the New World.* **New York: Atheneum, 1989.**
While 1492 was an exciting year for Spanish discovery, it was also the year that many Jews were expelled from Spain and Portugal. This book looks at some of their journey from Spain to the Americas.

Katz, Samuel M. *At Any Cost: National Liberation Terrorism.* **Minneapolis: Lerner Publications Company, 2004.**
This discussion of the history, formation, actions, and philosophies of a variety of different national liberation groups includes a chapter on the Basque group ETA.

Kneib, Martha. *Christopher Columbus: Master Italian Navigator in the Court of Spain.* **New York: Rosen Publishing Group, 2003.**
This biography describes the life and voyages of Columbus, including his exploration of the New World.

Márquez, Herón. *Latin Sensations.* **Minneapolis: Lerner Publications Company, 2001.**
Chart the rise of Latin pop stars, including Enrique Iglesias.

Meyer, Carolyn. *Isabel: Jewel of Castilla, Spain, 1466.* **New York: Scholastic, 2000.**
This is a fictionalized diary of young Isabel, who eventually became queen of Spain. In this book, an adolescent Isabel is forced to deal with her controlling half brother, King Enrique, and her younger, rebellious brother, King Alfonso.

Miklowitz, Gloria. *Secrets in the House of Delgado.* **Grand Rapids, MI: William B. Eerdmans Publishing, 2002.**
Set during the Spanish Inquisition, this novel features 14-year-old Maria, an orphan who is sent by the Catholic Church to spy on the Delgado family to determine if the family is practicing Judaism. As Maria becomes close to the family, she finds herself faced with a difficult decision.

Further Reading and Websites

Millar, Heather. *Spain in the Age of Exploration.* **New York: Benchmark Books, 1999.**
This work focuses on Spain and its explorations from the time of Columbus's discovery of the New World to the defeat of the Spanish Armada.

Pelta, Kathy. *Discovering Christopher Columbus.* **Minneapolis: Lerner Publications Company, 1991.**
This volume explores the ideas and biases historians have brought to the subject of Columbus's historic voyages and how historians have sorted the facts from the myths.

Ross, Nicholas, et al. *Miró.* **Hauppauge, NY: Barron's Juvenile, 1995.**
This biography covers the life and works of one of Spain's most famous modern artists, Joan Miró.

Si Spain
Website: <www.DocuWeb.ca/SiSpain/english/index.html>
This site looks at current affairs in Spain, as well as its historical and cultural development.

vgsbooks.com
Website: <http://www.vgsbooks.com>
Visit vgsbooks.com, the home page of the Visual Geography Series, which is updated frequently. You can get linked to all sorts of useful on-line information, including geographical, historical, demographic, cultural, and economic websites. The vgsbooks.com site is a great resource for late-breaking news and statistics.

Wojciechowska, Maia. *Shadow of a Bull.* **New York: Aladdin, 1992.**
In this novel, young Manolo Olivar is the son of one of Spain's greatest bullfighters. Manolo, however, is terrified of bulls. Somehow, he must find a way to keep his family's bullfighting tradition while pursuing his own dreams.

Worth, Richard. *The Spanish Inquisition in World History.* **Berkeley Heights, NJ: Enslow Publishers, 2002.**
Learn more about Spain's period of religious intolerance, which led to the expulsion of thousands of non-Catholics.

Index

Alfonso VI, King, 24
Alfonso XII, King, 31
Alfonso XIII, King, 31, 32
Almodóvar, Pablo, 53-54
Andalucians, 41
Andorra, 8, 10
animals, 17
architecture, 55–56. *See also* Calatrava, Santiago; Gaudí, Antoní
Atlantic Ocean, 8, 9, 10, 13, 14, 15
Aznar, José Maria, 7, 35, 36

Balearic Islands, 9, 13, 16, 73
Barcelona, 12, 16, 19, 72
Basques, 7, 34, 35–36, 40
Bilbao, 19
Black Death. *See* bubonic plague
Bonaparte, Napoleon, 30–31
bubonic plague, 26
bullfights, 47, 57

Calatrava, Santiago, 56
Canary Islands, 9, 10, 14,
Cantabrian Mountains, 10, 15, 17
Casals, Pablo, 52
Castilians, 41
Cataláns, 7, 40
Catalonia, 8, 10, 19, 40
Catholic Church, 33, 42, 46
Celts, 21-22
Ceuta, 9, 14
Charles, King, 28-29
Christianity, 22, 24, 28, 42-43
cities, 18-19, 39. *See also* Barcelona, Bilbao, Ceuta, Granada, La Coruña, Madrid, Melilla, Saragossa, Seville, Toledo, Valencia
civil war, 4, 32–33, 50-51
climate, 13, 15–16, 17
colonization, 28, 30
cultural life, 46–57
currency, 36, 65, 68

Dalí, Salvador, 55
dance, 51–52
de Cervantes Saavedra, Miguel, 50
de Rivera y Orbaneja, General Miguel Primo, 31–32
del Castillo, Antonio Cánovas, 31
Duero River, 15

Ebro River, 15
economy: 4, 19, 34, 58–65; agriculture, 5, 13, 17, 25, 59, 62–63; industry, 5, 18, 58, 61–62; services, 59-60; trade and tourism, 60–61; transportation and energy, 63–64
education, 45
El Greco, 54
environment, 17, 61
ethnic groups, 7, 13, 40–41. *See also* Basques, Jews, Moors, Roma
European Union (EU), 5, 35, 59
Euskadi ta Askatasuna (ETA), 34, 35–36. *See also* Basques

fauna, 17
Ferdinand, King, 26, 27, 28
Ferdinand VII, King, 31
film, 53–54
fine arts, 54–55
fishing, 62, 63
flag, 69
flora, 16
food, 48-49
France, 8, 30–31
Franco, General Francisco, 4, 32–34, 51, 70

Galicians, 41
Gaudí, Antoní, 56, 70
Gibraltar, 8, 13; Strait of, 9, 13, 14
González, Felipe, 35
government, 4, 36-37
Goya y Lucientes, Francisco, 54
Granada, 28, 72
Great Britain, 13, 29
Grís, Juan, 54
Guadalquivir River, 15, 19
Guadiana River, 15
Gypsies. *See* Roma

healthcare, 43–44
history, 4, 20–37: civil war, 4, 32-33; democracy, 34–36; early 1900s, 31-32; Franco regime, 4, 32–33; Habsburg rule, 28–29; Iberia, 20–22; Inquisition, 27; Moorish defeat, 25; Moorish rule, 23–25; parliamentary monarchy, 5, 37–38;

Reconquest, 24; Roman and Visigoth rule, 22–23; under French control, 30–31; War of Spanish Succession, 29 World War II, 33-34
holidays and festivals, 46-48

Iberian Peninsula, 8, 13, 20–21
Iglesias, Enrique, 52
Iglesias, Julio, 52
Iraq, war in, 7, 36
Isabella I, Queen, 26, 27, 28, 71
Islam, 23, 24, 43. *See also* Moors.

Jews, 24, 26, 27, 43; *See also* Spanish Inquisition
Juan Carlos, King, 34

La Coruña, 15
language, 13, 22, 40, 41, 43
literature, 49-51

Madrid, 13, 16, 18, 72
Majorca, 13, 14
Manzanares River, 18
maps, 6, 11
Mediterranean Sea, 8, 9, 10, 13, 15, 19, 21
Melilla, 9, 14
Meseta, 13, 15, 16
Miró, Joan, 55
Moors, 23–25, 28
mountains, 8, 10, 13, 15
Mulhacén, 13
Muñoz, Juan, 55
music, 51–53. *See also* Casals, Pablo; Iglesias, Enrique; Iglesias, Julio; national anthem

national anthem, 69
Nationalists, 32
natural resources, 17

Partida Socialista Obrero Español (PSOE), 35
people 38–45: education, 45; ethnic groups, 40–42; health, 43–45; language 43; religion, 42–43
Philip of Anjou, 29, 30
Phoenecians, 21-22
Picasso, Pablo, 54

Pico de Teide, 14
pollution, 17–18
Popular Front (Republican Army), 32–33
Popular Party, 35
population, 38–39
Portugal, 8, 15
Pyrenees Mountains, 8, 10, 15

religion, 22, 23, 26, 27, 28, 42–43: Jews in Spain, 24, 26, 27, 43; Muslims in Spain, 23, 24, 43; Roman Catholics in Spain, 27, 33, 42
rivers, 14–15, 18, 19
Roma, 41–42
rural life, 38, 39
Roman Catholic Church, 27, 33, 42

Saragossa, 19
Seville, 19
Spain: boundaries, size, and location, 4, 8–9; currency 36, 65, 68; fast facts, 68; flag, 69; maps, 6, 11; population, 38–39; timeline, 66–67
Spanish-American War, 31, 50
Spanish Armada, 29
Spanish Inquisition, 27
sports and recreation, 57

Tajo River, 15
Tápies, Antoni, 55
terrorism, 7, 34, 35–36, 60. *See also* Euskadi ta Askatasuna (ETA)
Toledo, 24, 72
topography, 9–14
tourism, 18, 19, 60–61
trade, 25, 60
transportation, 63–64

unemployment, 5
United States, 7, 31, 34

Velázquez, Diego, 54
Valencia, 12, 16, 19

War of Spanish Succession, 29–30
white storks, 17

Captions for photos appearing on cover and chapter openers:

Cover: Built in the sixteenth century, the Episcopal Palace and Museum in Albarracín draw tourists to this tiny town nestled in the Cantabrian Mountains.

pp. 4–5 The Alhambra, a majestic twelfth-century fortress built by the Moors, overlooks the city of Granada.

pp. 8–9 Jagged mountains adorn the skyline in the town of Montserrat in the Catalonia region of northeastern Spain.

pp. 20–21 Striped arches and tall columns crowd the interior of this Córdoba mosque. The Moors, an invading people from North Africa, left their stamp on Spain through language, culture, and especially through architecture.

pp. 38–39 Crowds of participants amble through the grounds of a market festival, or *feria*, in Jerez del Marquesado, near Granada.

pp. 46–47 Participants in the annual Running of the Bulls in Pamplona flee from a group of raging animals.

pp. 58–59 Since 2002 Spain has used the Euro as its national currency.

Photo Acknowledgments

The images in this book are used with the permission of: © Trip/J. Randall, pp. 4–5, 16; Digital Cartographics, pp. 6, 11; © Francesc Muntada/CORBIS, pp. 8–9; © Trip/TH-Foto Werbung, p. 10; © Trip/A. Tovy, pp. 12, 51; © Trip/C. Toms, p. 13; © Trip/B. Turner, pp. 14, 42, 60, 63; © Trip/H. Rodgers, pp. 15, 20–21, 22, 40, 48, 62, 64; © Trip/M.Feeney, pp. 17, 44; © Galyn C. Hammond, pp. 18, 23, 54; © A.A.M. Van Der Heyden/Independent Picture Service, pp. 19, 52 (top), 56; © Trip/C. Rennie, pp. 24, 57 (top); © Gianni Dagli Orti/CORBIS, p. 25; Museo del Prado, p. 27; © North Wind Pictures, pp. 28 (both), 31; The Art Archive/Society of Apothecaries/Eileen Tweedy, p. 29; The Art Archive/Musée du Louvre Paris/Dagli Orti, p. 30; © Hulton-Deutsch Collection/CORBIS, p. 32 (top); Illustrated London News, pp. 32 (bottom), 33; © AFP/CORBIS, pp. 36, 37, 46–47, 53; © Trip/Eric Smith, pp. 38–39; © Trip/B. Gadsby, p. 41; © Trip/Ask Images, p. 45; © Dan Herrick/Zuma Press, p. 52 (bottom); © Trip/Chris Belcher, p. 55; © Trip/R. Belbin, p. 57 (bottom); Todd Strand/Independent Picture Service, pp. 58–59, 68; Laura Westlund, p. 69.

Cover: © Francesc Muntada/CORBIS. Back cover: NASA.